First Published 2009
© Send and Ripley History Society 2009
© Clare McCann – Editor
All Rights Reserved

Send and Ripley History Society
Send Manor
Send Marsh Green
Woking
Surrey
GU23 6JS

ISBN 978-0-9562929-0-2

Printed and bound by Taurus Print & Design Limited

Front cover photograph - Michael Morris and his younger brother.

THIS COLLECTION OF WAR MEMORIES WAS BEGUN TO MARK THE 60TH ANNIVERSARY OF THE ENDING OF THE SECOND WORLD WAR.

Further memories have been added since and the Society hopes others will be recorded for posterity.

The Send and Ripley History Society would like to thank all those who contributed to the book, sometimes at the cost of reviving painful memories.

We would like to dedicate this book to all those on the Home Front, who lived through the war in Send and Ripley and whose contribution is perhaps overshadowed by those who served in the armed forces. It is our aim in due course to produce a second book, dedicated to those who gave their lives and who are commemorated on the Send and Ripley war memorials.

THE MEMORIES OF

RITA AVERY NÉE SHOESMITH

At the outbreak of the war I lived in Filbert Cottage in Ripley High Street near the entrance to the Green, but I ended the war living in Newark Lane and that was because a bomb destroyed our house. On Saturday 30th November 1940 my parents' friends had been playing whist but fortunately they had left. I had a premonition that something was going to happen but my brother Den and I had gone to bed. There was a lot of overhead activity that night and we got to recognise a Junkers German bomber by the tone of the engine. Just before 11 o'clock a bomb from an aircraft reduced our house to a heap of rubble. My father was blown down into the cellar and pinned down by a large beam, my mother managed to shelter under our dining room table, my brother ended up in the crater and lost the seat of his pyjamas and I was trying to get under my bed but was covered with rubble and trapped by a wardrobe and rubble from the roof. I recall the playing cards from the whist drive floating in the air and later seeing a dress wrapped round the chimney. Luckily we all survived and I even found my doll in one piece.

Filbert Cottage

My older brother, Pete, who was with the army in Liss, came home on the Sunday and got a lift from Guildford station but had no idea that we had been bombed. He was terribly shocked as he found a pile of rubble where once the house had stood.

After the bombing we lived with an aunt in Grove Heath for a while but, on looking back, she was not that kind to us, and my Mum and I practically camped out at the Guildford Borough Council offices to try to get us rehoused. They eventually requisitioned a house in Newark Lane, Wisteria Cottage, where I live now. The reason it was empty was that it formed part of the old workhouse, and the adjacent cottage had been bombed and the people had left. There was also bomb damage at the front and back of what later became the Suzuki garage (now closed) and two cottages in Newark Lane, 'Little Horrells', were destroyed. Later a doodlebug (the German V1 flying missile) fell on Dunsborough Fields – I remember that my mother was ill in bed and I had done the washing and the sheets were in a galvanised iron bath. The explosion brought down a lot of soot and I had to wash everything again.

The food during the war was sometimes horrible; in particular I remember scrambled eggs that were made from dried egg. On one occasion my mother was showing us the one piece of corned beef that she had to share between the four of us, when our dog jumped up and ate it! I also recall that once a week I used to queue in Quarry Street, Guildford, for a pound of sausages – they were horrid but we were grateful for them. Mother used to take them out of their skins and spice them up or sometimes curry them.

If we heard the siren when we were at school we got under our desks. Later, they built shelters in the playground and we had little chairs in them but the

House that replaced Filbert Cottage

shelters were cold. We also had chairs in a cupboard under our stairs, which we used as a shelter. These stairs were turned over when the bomb hit our house. I remember once, after I had been home for lunch, I was walking back to school when I saw a plane flying low over the village. We came to recognise different types of planes and I knew this was a German plane and it started to strafe the village and I ran into the churchyard to take shelter.

We had evacuees at our school. They were from London and I remember them queuing up outside the church hall, which was on the site of what is now Clifford James, with their cases and their gas masks. Mother had one of them round to tea, and I am still in touch with an evacuee who now lives in Southampton.

There were quite big guns on the Broadmead and we could see the tracer bullets going up into the sky. Sometimes bits of shrapnel would fall in the garden and we could hear them hitting the old tin roof on our shed.

Later in the war we saw a Junkers German bomber dropping its bombs in the direction of the Vickers factory, where my brother worked as a draughtsman.

He used to drive there in a little Austin 7 and that night he was very late home, which made us worried but it turned out he had been ferrying injured people to hospital. Another German plane came down in Ockham and I pedalled over to see the wreck. The Canadians who were based over there took the pilot to Dr Creet, and then I think he was taken to Woking police station. He may have ended up in Merrow, where there was a Prisoner of War camp.

There was still some entertainment and in particular I recall the sixpenny 'hops' (dances) and the cinematograph shows in the old church hall. We sometimes saw rats in the hall and if the film broke down we all used to stamp our feet.

Towards the end of the war I worked for the Ministry of Agriculture in a section that dealt with drainage. I was there when the war ended and my mother and I went up to London for VE day. She was a real royalist! The streets were packed; you could hardly shuffle but it was very friendly.

Sadly Rita Avery has died since recording this memory.

THE MEMORIES OF

JOHN MERCER - EVACUEE

My memories are of the period 1940-1941 – so I would have been about twelve years old.

After the first appearance of the Luftwaffe over Spithead to lay mines, the Portsmouth authorities executed a second evacuation of youngsters and this included a group of us from Solent View Road in Drayton. The phoney war for mainland England was now over.

The chosen location for us was what turned out to be the most delightful village in the county of Surrey: Ripley – so peaceful and rural then -only twenty miles south of London and in a direct flight path from Northern France. Extremely well thought out!

After a couple of moves I was billeted under the care of a dear lady named Mrs Perrin of 4 Hedgecroft Cottages. Such lovely jam tarts and steamed puddings – and she looked after me very well.

School was attended locally in a building that no longer exists, under the headmastership of Fred Dixon, a delightful man who had us do an awful lot of gardening, if not much in the way of mathematics. I visited him on occasions right up to his death, and my wife and I attended his funeral. Most of us Pompey-ites boosted the membership of the local church by joining the choir. After several months, however, I left Decani 3[1] following a dispute with the incumbent over my alleged bad behaviour – even though I was dressed like an angel. We could earn two and a half pence in old money by attending both services on a Sunday, Evensong during the week and choir practice. My voice broke anyway!

Ripley lads challenged the Portsmouth lot to the inevitable game of cricket on their noted village green. They won the toss and, in fairness, declared quite early. I forget the total number of runs but the game continued even when they realised what a hopeless lot we were. The challenge was never repeated, understandably, but we had begun to fit in quite favourably, and I would not be surprised if some friendships made then still exist. My old autograph book has several names in it.

Three further new activities: during the warm summer learning to swim (successfully) in the River Wey, with Tom Sawyer-like enthusiasm and excitement. Enjoyed, too, was the purchase of fishing tackle from a shop (long gone) and silent hours spent in daydreaming – but never to catch a blessed thing! I wonder if anyone else remembers using a bubble pipe to smoke the product of a bush, which grew in the village and looked like white tobacco.

[1] Presumably the name of the choir

There were a few evacuees from other places, e.g. Croydon. Eric Chester and Eric Strange I recall quite well – but we never met afterwards.

A building in Newark Lane (Lutidine House) was occupied as a school for girls. I had a short schoolboy crush at the time on Patricia Clapton[2]. I discovered, when calling on her many years later, she'd thought I was just a 'square'. Ah me…

The period of the Battle of Britain is recorded in detail elsewhere. However, I distinctly remember the lunchtime raid on Vickers and seeing 'planes and smoke in the distance. One 'plane, easily distinguished as German, came over Newark Lane, quite low – it was in fact crashing. All the plumes of smoke from shell bursts were fading but one white patch remained. It was a parachute drifting down. At least one member of the crew survived, to be treated in the doctor's surgery, then opposite the school. Mr Townsend, next-door neighbour, was injured in this raid.

Other recollections are of seeing barrage balloons go up in flames, caught in an electric storm. Even as a young lad I thought of the Graf Zeppelin. I remember long convoys of lorries traversing Newark Lane at night, coming and going from goodness knows where. Also I heard mobile Bofors anti-aircraft guns firing at night at what seemed to be close proximity to Mrs Perrin's front door.

I also remember watching the blacksmith shoeing horses in the centre of the village in a building now 'restored' and its origins completely unrecognisable.

Can anyone remember the name of "Sir Tiffy-Cate", who promenaded through the village one day during Spitfire Week? The prize was a 15/-d (75p) National Savings Certificate. Incidentally, the £5000 necessary was raised to buy a Spitfire fighter plane, a very good show.

One morning in the area across the road and into the estate beyond No 4 were hundreds of strips of a very fragile, thin black paper-like material, about one inch wide and six or eight inches long. Dropped during the night – by whom? Long before 'window' was disclosed.[3]

School-leaving age was fourteen in those days, so I left Ripley to return home, then on the Isle of Wight, after spending such a pleasant and memorable episode in my early and formative years. I then continued my education in Cowes.

[2] Almost certainly Eric Clapton's mother
[3] Window was shiny reflective strip designed to confuse enemy radar

THE MEMORIES OF

GERALD CHANDLER, HIS WIFE JOAN NÉE HATCHER AND HER SISTER LILLIAN POWELL

At the outbreak of war Gerald was 10 years old and living at Homeleigh, Portsmouth Road, Ripley, where he had moved to from Wisley. He remembers a test siren when he was still at Wisley but thinks that at the beginning of the war 'Turp' Giles used to cycle around the village giving warnings. Eventually there was a siren on the fire station (now the Scout Hut).

Although he realises now all the awful things that happened during the war, as a young boy Gerald viewed the war as exciting and a bit of an adventure. Fairly early in the war he recalled that as he was cycling to Send from Ripley for a woodwork class, he and his friend stopped at Send Marsh to watch the air activity over Vickers. A Heinkel was shot down and crashed at Long Reach, Ockham. They decided to skip their class and cycle to Ockham, where the Canadians would not allow them through but eventually they were allowed to see the wreck. Lillian Powell says they saw the pilot swinging down on his parachute and she felt sorry for him. Her sister Joan was watching through the railings in Ripley and saw the injured pilot brought to Dr

Creet in Ripley, where a big crowd had gathered. She said he looked petrified. She was not sure what became of him but rumour had it that he died before reaching Guildford Hospital (St Lukes).

Gerald, Joan and Lillian all remember the concrete shelters at the school. They had brick fronts and earth banked up around them. They thought Norcon might have made the shelters, like the one now at the Ripley Museum.

The children used the shelters during the day and the locals brought their bedding and used them at night. They remembered Mrs Hill (Aunt Lily) bringing a deckchair to sleep in. For a while a London couple, who were afraid of

Canadian soldiers in Surrey

sleeping in London, used to travel down every night to Ripley and slept in the Hatchers' home, 3 Grandis Cottages, while the Hatcher family were in the shelter. Eventually, locals got fed up and returned to sleeping at home but Mr and Mrs Smithers and Mr and Mrs Lloyd slept on the floor and they all agreed that there was a feeling that if everyone kept together then they would be safe.

Norcon shelter from Newark Lane now at the museum

They all had memories of various bombs that fell in and around the village - a string of bombs that fell on Humphreys' farm at Grove Heath and incendiaries on Polesden Lane. In Ripley itself, bombs fell in front of the present Suzuki Garage, that was then a snack bar, and in the yard, on Little Horrells in Newark Lane and on a cottage on the other side of the lane but left the snack bar untouched.

There was also the bomb that destroyed Filbert Cottage (see Rita Avery's account) but after that the village was relatively quiet until the doodlebug attacks. Lillian remembers cycling in the dark when a 'buzz bomb' came over and the engine cut out. She got down in the ditch with a terrified young boy, who was on the way to his first day at work. The bomb fell on the Broadmead but the boy was too frightened to go on and she sent him home to his mother.

Joan moved on from Ripley School to St Bede's and she recalls that trenches were dug round the playing field and they sheltered there to protect them from blast. They all remembered the doodlebug that fell at Burnt Common and killed several members of the Privett family. Gerald had left school by then and was working at Fisher's Garage. A fellow worker, Don Parsons, heard the blast and dived under a car that was on axle stands. Luckily it did not collapse on him but he was very frightened. The Wrights, who lived next door to the Privetts, had to move out and went to Grove Heath North. Their house there was also damaged by a doodlebug but luckily it hit a large oak, which saved the houses from worse damage.

Gerald Chandler pointed out that there were very few cars on the roads and petrol was rationed, so although they had some car maintenance work at the garage, they also assembled Valentine tank wheels for the War Department.

Local women also assembled rubber bushes for tanks and some of this work was done at home. All single women over a certain age had to undertake some war work. Even Lillian, who had a young baby, worked in Pyrford on inspection of components of Wellington bombers. Prior to this, she had six weeks at Vickers and she thought it was hell – dark and horrible. She recalled that while she was at work she heard a doodlebug explode and she was worried about her baby but she could not ring home as very few people had telephones in those days. They rang Collins the bakers, who were able to tell her that it had fallen on the Green but the blast blew out the windows of Wellers. Close by to where she worked in Pyrford was the Rowley Bristow Hospital, which housed wounded soldiers, who were dressed in blue – there was little else there then and all the housing was built later.

They all had recollections of the Canadians who were stationed in the area. There was a camp at Ockham Park and the Canadians would come into the village to drink but they were always well behaved. They brought in Coca-Cola, cigarettes, nylons and chocolate which was popular. The billiard table at the Legion was moved out so they could dance with local girls. Families would invite one or two Canadians over for Christmas. Some of the soldiers were young and handsome but Mrs Powell seemed to remember that her parents invited one who was older and quieter. She could not remember what they fed

them on but they did not have turkey. The Canadians often brought things with them and when they passed in the street they always waved but suddenly in the run up to D-Day they were gone without warning.

Needless to say there were food shortages during the war but people got by. They had the bare essentials but supplemented rations with rabbits, pheasants and pigeons, which might have been poached. Families kept chickens or ducks and grew vegetables and tried to be self-sufficient. They ate bread and dripping and Gerald recalled that Mrs Figgers brought dripping into them at Fishers garage and he is convinced that she skimmed it off the swill that she cooked up for her pigs at Warren Farm. Children did not have squash or fruit drinks and they all hated sweet rationing. Mrs Jackman was the cook at St Bede's School and she cooked things like cheese pastry, sausage and mash, bacon pudding and stew. For 'afters' they had watery custard and chocolate sponge cake and apples when in season.

School children got a week off in October to go potato picking for which they were paid 4d an hour. Joan chose to work at Guinness's as they paid 1/- an hour. They also picked fruit at Wisley and for Arthur Hill, who had land opposite the kennels and on Georgelands and grew peas. Mr Dixon at Ripley School encouraged children to 'Dig for Victory' and they grew vegetables behind the police station but they never knew what happened to the vegetables!

They had a line of pennies on the kerb as a fundraiser and they were also encouraged to buy 6d and 2/6d savings stamps. Mr Hatcher used to go round to his neighbours selling these stamps. There were also shows in the old village hall, put on by The Ripples, to raise money to build shelters.

Gerald said that they used to collect pieces of shrapnel and swop them – the most prized item was the nose cone of a shell. They would go out looking for debris, which was probably dangerous as there were unexploded incendiaries around. The boys knew all the different types of planes flying over and he

DIG FOR VICTORY LEAFLET
NUMBER 19 (NEW SERIES)

remembers seeing planes streaming over towing gliders at the time of D-Day. Joan Chandler said she and a friend were at the Savoy cinema at Cobham on VE Day when the manager came on stage and made the announcement and everyone cheered. They got on their bikes and rode back to Ripley. She made the point that during the war they rode everywhere on bikes as the roads were very empty. Gerald said you could roller skate all the way from Ripley to

Burpham, although you needed to take oil to lubricate the wheels. Getting back to VE Day in Ripley, pianos from the White Hart and the Ship were brought outside and there was dancing in the street. The manager at Ockham Mill, where she worked, gave her and the other staff 5/- as a present. Gerald said he and others went out and about setting off thunderflashes, which his father had got for them from Vickers.

They all agreed that the celebrations for VJ Day were not so big in Ripley and that they found the news of the atom bomb hard to comprehend, with news that one bomb had wiped out a whole city and that people had been consumed by the blast.

THE MEMORIES OF

JACK MALLENDER

Some factories such as Vickers Aircraft raised their own defence forces and as I was working there I joined VA Force. It was much the same as the Home Guard – uniforms, arms and duties.

Later it was decided to disband the VA Force and those who wished could transfer to their local Home Guard. I joined Ripley Home Guard – Major Kay at the Kilns was in charge. The Home Guard was originally the Local Defence Volunteers, which was known as 'Look Duck and Vanish!'

A Blacker Bombard was mounted on the Green, much like a mortar (sited towards Dunsborough). The barrel was approximately 18 inches long and 6 inches in diameter with a spigot in the centre down which the bomb was loaded – stand back and duck! I never saw it fired.

Ripley Home Guard used the large room at the Talbot for an HQ – talks and instruction. Ripley Green was the scene for parades and exercises.

Call outs during the night hours did happen, but thankfully not too often. The practice was that someone banged on the door – 'Call Out' – everything was lying ready (always) then off to 'Call' my allotted members. I must say the turn out was very good.

Ripley Home Guard on the Green

Several of us Guardees had the opportunity to go to Bisley range to qualify in marksmanship – we all passed and were awarded the crossed-rifle badge, after which a team was raised to shoot against other companies in friendly competition!

It was arranged to do a night patrol to Wisley Airfield. Sergeant Bert Freeman was in charge (Bert was a local postman, ex-army, a grand chap) so about 16 of some of the brave and the bold went forth along the Portsmouth Road, up Ogden Hill and on past turnings right and left (no signboards) but Hark! Listen! Engine running and a clattering noise!

Sergeant signalled a halt, listened some more, then with a wave we moved into the trees alongside the airfield. Next – open order - the airfield was somewhat higher ground than where we were, so it gave some cover as we moved forward. Having moved in and more or less surrounded the moving machine, it was brought to a stop. And then surprise, surprise – Percy Chandler gang-mowing the grass runway!! Now Percy always said what he thought, such as 'Why don't you silly… go home to bed and leave me to get on' and so on. It made sense: with aircraft using the runway during the day, friend Percy had to mow during the dark.

Another exercise we went on was really a watching brief. There was a lane that went from Portsmouth Road, where the Wisley Airfield entrance now is, to Ockham. At Ockham the lane was wide enough for farm traffic with trees overhanging the lane and to this area we were taken. How? Very likely in an army lorry. Having arrived, the orders were to 'Get behind the hedge both sides, no smoking, no talking – you are here to watch'. This was done and everyone settled down. It became a bit boring just waiting for 'What?' Now and again there was a 'Quiet there' or 'Shhh'. Eventually

Ripley Home Guard on the Green

lorries were heard turning into the lane and as they passed under the trees it happened… From the trees dropped Canadian troops and set about (friendly, I hope) troops in the lorries. Phew! How long they had been in the trees I really don't know, we had been there for hours. This exercise showed what could be done using natural camouflage.

MARGARET (PEGGY) METHOLD NÉE PARROTT

The Parrott family moved to Ripley from Lightwater in 1936. Peggy's father was a policeman and they moved into the new police houses (no. 2). Sergeant Tickner was in charge and in one of the other cottages was a policeman who used a motorbike. During the war there were vegetable gardens behind the cottages maintained by the schoolboys and they had to come through the Parrotts' garden to get to them. Her father had all sorts of extra responsibilities during the war – for example helping to enforce the blackout. She recalled hearing banging and clattering outside their house and discovered the edges of the pavement were being painted white to make things safer at night.

Air raid alerts were phoned through to the police station and sometimes the calls were diverted to their house if he was off duty. She recalls her father putting his gun on the table when having his tea, which made her feel uncomfortable. (Apparently policemen were armed during the war). She also remembered that her father had to collect a German airman, shot down in Ockham, and bring him to Dr Creet's for treatment. The airman had been shot through the foot and his boot was passed round the locals to make a collection for the war effort!

Peggy and Bill Parrott

Harry, Peggy's brother (known as Bill) and Peggy had been born in Horley. She went to Woking Grammar School and when she left school she had to report to the Juvenile Employment Bureau as the war had already broken out.

She was given no choice of employment and found herself as a lab assistant at Guildford Technical College, despite

Bill Parrott, left, in front of his plane

never having done much science. She earned 15 shillings a week and was able to move to a receptionist job at the college after about a year.

Her brother, who was four years her senior, started as trainee surveyor with Surrey County Council at Kingston in 1939. He was encouraged to enlist even before the war and he joined the RAF Volunteer Reserve. He had had only about one month's training when war broke out. He became a Sergeant Observer flying in Blenheim bombers, which meant navigating and bomb aiming. He told his sister how it worried him when they overshot the mark when dropping bombs, as he knew it would mean civilian casualties. He was based at Thorney Island flying missions into France and sadly was killed in an accident when returning in bad weather in December 1940 and was possibly the first fatality from Ripley. The bad news

was rung through to Ripley Police station and Peggy's father came to collect her from work. She drove with her father to Rowledge, the family home, to collect her uncle and then they drove to Thorney Island where Mr Parrott had to identify the body.

Bill was given an RAF funeral, with the coffin draped in a Union Jack but, as the Parrotts had moved around, they did not want him buried in Ripley, not knowing if they would stay, so he was buried in Rowledge. Many people came from Ripley and the Reverend Morgan Thomas of Ripley took the service.

Peggy's mother had helped found the WI in Ripley and when the siren went off on the Sunday that war broke out she had gone off to the Red Cross Centre in her green overall – fortunately her services were not needed that day. Mrs Parrott was naturally deeply affected by her son's death and in 1942 she developed throat cancer and the doctor felt this had been brought on by the tragedy. Despite her illness she got no extra rations although swallowing was so difficult. She received treatment at the Farnham Road hospital and the vicar often took her, as her father was on duty and so few people had cars or fuel (petrol was rationed to 5 gallons a month). Her father had bought a Hillman Minx in 1938, which he garaged at Bland's Garage, but used a bicycle when on duty. He was called to the hospital in the middle of the night and had to cycle as his car was locked in the garage. Mrs Methold knew her mother must have died as her father returned home with his wife's handbag on the handlebars.

Another consequence of her brother's tragic death was meeting her future husband. Apparently Tyndall Methold, a solicitor in Guildford, and his brother Ken, who helped run the family garage on the Portsmouth Road, went to cheer up the Parrotts after Bill was killed and Peggy, who had not met Ken before, eventually married him in 1942. They were married in Ripley Church. It was a white wedding but, due to the war, the dress was borrowed. She had three bridesmaids whose dresses were made

Celebrating the end of petrol rationing

of curtain material, as this was not rationed. Her farsighted future mother-in-law had stockpiled dried fruit prior to rationing (for her three children) so she was able to have a wedding cake. They lived in a flat in a barn on the end of the garage.

During the war over half of the workshop was given over to munitions production and they turned out washers, brackets, etc., for the arms industry and employed about 12 people. Her father-in-law ran the nightshift and was allowed fuel to drive the employees back to their digs in Guildford. Ken managed the day shift. One night a fight broke out between a Czech woman called Lotti, who had had a hard time in a POW camp, and another female employee. The police were called and the two women were taken away to Guildford. The other woman never returned and they were told she was a spy! After that they were all very wary and someone remarked to Mr Methold that if Hitler ever won the war then his name would be on his list.

Peggy told us that there was little civilian traffic on the road during the war because of fuel rationing, whereas before the war her father had had to don white armlets to control the traffic at the junction of the

High Street and Newark Lane. She said on wartime Sundays it was so quiet that children would play marbles on the white lines on the road. Also the gypsies held horse sales near the Jovial Sailor and they would run the horses up and down the road.

Not directly related to the war, she mentioned that the Metholds had come to the village from Bramley in 1926 and had built the garage. The holes for the fuel tanks had to be excavated by hand. A visiting tramp, who lodged in a barn at the Jovial Sailor, had got stuck in the clay whilst digging and had finally been extricated using a steam tractor.

To conclude the story of the Parrott family, her father's unmarried sister came to keep house after her mother's death. Two years later Mr Parrott remarried. He married Mrs Best from Newark Mill and he retired from the police in 1945. He had to leave the police house and they lived for sometime in the little hut adjacent to the mill before moving to a cottage next to Greens hardware store where he eventually died. Years later when Greens was destroyed in a fire and the cottage was damaged, Peggy lost many treasures from her childhood. After the war Peggy and Ken built one of the first bungalows in Boughton Hall Avenue, which prior to that had been wartime agricultural land. Although this took time, due to shortages of bricks etc, they were able to move in with their young son in 1946.

MEMORIES FROM

JOHN HUTSON

John was 10 years old when war broke out and was with his gang of friends on a railway bridge at East Clandon when they saw many trains laden with children wearing labels – only when he got home did he realise that war had been declared and that the children were being evacuated from London. Later in the war, when his parents had moved from 2 Rawridge Cottages, Portsmouth Road, to 2 Georgelands, his parents had a family billeted on them but John did not take a lot of notice, as this was not exceptional at the time.

At the outset of the war he was at Ripley School and he remembers occasions when children marched through the village to the Methodist Hall. This was used as additional teaching space as school numbers had been swollen by the evacuees. When shelters were built in the playground Mr Dixon put him, with others, in charge of keeping younger boys in order. He does not think he was a prefect but was chosen just because he was large for his age – sufficiently so to warrant extra clothing coupons.

He recalled the day when he was carrying out his duties at the school shelter when a German pilot was shot down and brought to Dr Creet's surgery for treatment – like Mr Chandler, he too heard a rumour that the Canadians saw to it that the pilot did not survive – although it seems this was just a rumour!

John moved on to the newly opened St Bede's. He does not recall shelters there and says they went out into the field if there was a raid, presumably to avoid flying glass but it hardly seems very safe. He said that in his spare time he, like many others, raised rabbits and chickens. At one time he thinks he had more than 60 rabbits in his back garden. He supplied his rabbits to butchers, including Conisbees, for meat

and to others as pets. His reputation for rearing livestock was obviously known at school because the then Head, Ben Gay, got him to help when he decided to introduce rabbits and chickens at school. Unfortunately he decided to keep them in the central quadrangle and they tended to escape into the corridors!

John's father's health had been destroyed by his service in World War 1 and he was unable to work much. His mother had many nursing and caring jobs locally but she was keen for John to leave school to earn a living and to contribute to the family finances. He had hoped to train as a carpenter at Barretts, where he had spent spare time as a boy helping out, but by the time he left school, aged 13, Barretts had been given over to manufacturing munitions and so he took on gardening jobs including work at the Talbot Hotel. He told me that the landlord of the Talbot had gone into the Navy but his wife ran the business with the help of an Italian chef, Mr Petrozzini. He was an excellent cook but, due to his nationality, he had to report weekly to the police station.

When John was not at work, he was very involved with the local scouts who met at Dunsborough under the leadership of Alf Blakeman. Later in the war they moved to the Church Hall, which became the scout hut, near the modern day Clifford James. The scouts were practice casualties for the newly formed ARP and the Red Cross. The ARP, run by Mr Young, the first Chief Officer, was based in an empty cottage in White

Horse Yard before moving to a purpose built building on the edge of the Green, next to which was a large water tank for extinguishing fires. Their vehicles were kept in old farm buildings. The Red Cross used the same premises at White Horse Yard and was run by Mrs Rose and Mrs Pitondreau (?). The senior scouts rode round the village blowing whistles to warn of an air raid, although this was only until a siren was organised. Apparently church bells were also used on occasions. The scouts also salvaged bottles, bones and newspapers and stored them at their hut until they were collected for recycling. He said local railings, including those in front of the Vicarage, went to the war effort.

John talked of the high level of attacks on Ripley and wonders if it was because German planes dropped their bombs going in or out of London. There were barrage balloons between Ripley and Weybridge, a machine gun nest on the Green manned by the Home Guard and searchlights at Hungry Hill Farm as well as guns on the Broadmead. The local Home Guard were based at the rear of the Talbot in sheds and a pill box was built on Lamberts Hill on the road out of Ripley, not to mention the Canadians in Ockham Park (many of whom went on the Dieppe raid, never to return). He feels these defences may have caused German planes to home-in on Ripley. He mentioned bomb attacks that are covered elsewhere in this book, but in particular he recalled a string of bombs that landed on the Green, in Newark

Lane, in the High Street and on the tennis court of Chapel Farm, miraculously causing no loss of life.

Due to petrol rationing there was almost no private road traffic and people depended on walking, cycling and local buses. There was a Blue Saloon bus every 30 minutes to Guildford and also a London General bus to Kingston every half hour. The 436 went hourly to Woking but the Greenline to London was eventually cancelled, presumably to conserve fuel. Fuel shortages also meant best use had to be made of local carriers. John said Doug White, who ran a coal merchants behind the old school (now the Legion) in Rose Lane, used his two drivers, Mr Cox and Mr Chandler, to transport goods to Horsley and Clandon as well as delivering coal (which was incidentally also rationed).

John's career as a gardener did not last long due to a fortuitous visit to the Ripley pharmacy. Kenneth White had recently taken over the pharmacy and was

impressed when John knew enough to reject Solution Tablets as a substitute for Tannic Acid Jelly, and ended up offering him a job, which was to turn out to be a lifelong career. John said the landlady at the Talbot made no trouble about him leaving and even asked him back to a staff dinner. The Ripley pharmacy became renowned later in the war for making penicillin, when

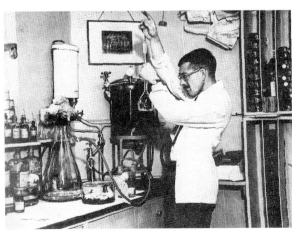

Kenneth White in his pharmacy

John Hutson

antibiotics were in their infancy.

Finally, John told of his postwar role as leader of a team to reinstate the northeast end of the Green. During the war the land had been taken over by the Surrey War Agriculture Commission, based at Ockham Church Farm, and tractors had yanked trees out of the ground to clear it for crops. The Commission had promised to reinstate the land after the war but this was not done and, when they pulled out, the Simmonds family at Dunsborough continued to farm the land.

Eventually it was no longer farmed but was cordoned off with an electric fence. John and others protested to the Parish Council and discovered that, not only was a modern day enclosure taking place but also no rent was being paid. John and his 'Volunteers' were not prepared to let the lack of money get in their way and with Sunday morning work sessions, they eventually replanted the trees.

Surrey Villager 18th April 1972.

'DIGGING FOR VICTORY' — 30 YEARS ON

THE drive by residents of Ripley to reclaim all the land that was originally the village green, one of the largest in the country, continues. Half of it was ploughed and planted with arable crops during the Second World War under the "Dig for Victory" policy, and now, 30 years later, part of it is still under cultivation.

A group of about 80 villagers, known locally as The Volunteers, have restored about two-thirds of the land that was ploughed up. They are now awaiting a go-ahead from Ripley Parish Council to start work on the remaining third.

In a letter to the "Villager", Mr. Frank Brown, of Honeysuckle Cottage, Newark Lane, Ripley, explains how The Volunteers came to be formed.

He writes, "In March, 1970, at the annual parish meeting, Mr. John Hutson proposed the re-establishment of the area of Ripley Green which had been under cultivation since the 'Dig for Victory' policy . . . Mr. Hutson had as a boy helped in the uprooting of trees and levelling of ground and was assured, as was the rest of the village, that this would be restored soon after the ending of hostilities.

"This area had been a mixture of gorse, rough grass, silver birch, oak and alder coppice, and a variety of wild flowers and undergrowth . . . Owing to various policies pursued at county and village level, Dunsborough Farm had retained its right to crop this area as it chose . . .

"The parish council, while it agreed that Mr. Hutson's proposal was, in the main, reflecting public opinion, raised many obstacles, including the familiar spectre of cost to the ratepayer and the fact that . . . labour in the form of hard sweat would be most unlikely to be forthcoming. However, the proposals were accepted in principle, the details to be arranged later by the chairman of the council, Mr. John Paul.

Mr. Brown said that by November of that year the coun-cil had arranged with Duns-borough Farm to take back con-trol of a section of the green to attempt to re-establish the natural plant and animal life. It decided there were sufficient saplings within the coppice at the end of the green for transplant-ing, and it was understood that this operation would be at no cost to Ripley ratepayers.

He said The Volunteers had spent many an enjoyable and back-breaking Sunday morning replanting saplings, tree seedlings, and bracken besides cleaning and maintaining footpaths.

He continued, "Many others have expressed great willingness to take part in any future work which might be proposed by the council . . . It is truly a village affair, carried out with the grea-test of good humour and camara-derie, much to the chagrin of those cynics who believe that where two or three are gathered together strife can be the only result.

"The decision has already been taken to revert the half not yet restored to its former self, but the machinery of government, as of God, grinds exceeding slow if exceeding fine, and The Volunteers are still awaiting their starting orders . . ."

Mr. Brown regards the work as important in encouraging bird life and small mammals to return to the green and also in offset-ting the harmful effects on wild life caused by the spread of suburbia and intensive farming.

He told the "Villager" that since restoration work started stonechats, bullfinches, and rab-bits had returned, and they hoped that weasels, stoats, badgers, foxes, warblers, and birds of prey would come back.

MEMORIES FROM

SID STANLEY

I was about 12 years old when war broke out and living at 3 Tannery Lane, Send. On September 3rd when war was declared, the air raid siren went off and all the residents of 1–5 Tannery Lane and, I think, the Challens and Mr Sale, congregated at the top of the lane looking for German planes!

Late in 1939 we moved to 9 Mays Corner and I went to Send School on Send Hill and then to St Bede's for a few months before leaving school at 14. I went to work at May and Hardy's (where Fishers Garage was along the Portsmouth Road) and we made parts for the aircraft industry.

My father joined the Auxiliary Fire Service. The fire station was next to the Manor House in a garage owned by Gordon Stewart. There was a fire engine and a Dennis fire pump. When Dad was on duty we went back and stayed with relatives in Tannery Lane. One night we had got as far as Broomfields (later the pharmacy and now Walnut Tree Place) when we heard a whistling sound and a bomb landed in the gardens of 11 and 12 Mays Corner. Dad went back and, of about 19 people in the two houses, only one was injured and he had put his hand on the range and burnt his hand. Our house had only one broken window and Dad found our two lodgers safely

sheltering under the table. The bomb or landmine made a huge crater and all sorts of people from the army or air force came and measured it.

I remember another bomb fell on the Rec., probably on the penalty spot! Then there were the flying bombs (also known as doodlebugs). One day Harold Parrott and I left work and cycled up to the crossroads (there was no roundabout then at Burnt Common) we turned right to go down Stiles Hill (now Send Barns Lane) when we heard a flying bomb coming. Before we could decide what to do, the engine stopped and we were thrown off our bikes by the blast and we ended up in the ditch. There was an old man, I think he was called Mr Turner, who was also thrown in the ditch and we pulled him out. The bomb had caused a red fog from brick dust. An American convoy came down the road and stopped. They would not let us cross the road but a whole family had been killed except one who was not at home (see Gilbert Privett's memories). I was very lucky. Another flying bomb hit a tree at the bottom of the road going into Send and I think it exploded and killed one man.

There was a Royal Engineers bomb disposal unit based at Heath House (near Cartbridge), Canadians based in

Air Training Corps at St Bede's. (Note some of the younger recruits are not yet in uniform).

Woking, Ockham Park and Newlands Corner and ammo dumps all over the place. The Canadians used the ponds off Potters Lane to test their vehicles to see if they were waterproof, in preparation for D-Day and they also built a pontoon bridge across the largest pond. There were also soldiers on the Broadmead. I remember one time early in the war we were fishing on Tannery Bridge when we saw a single soldier running across the Broadmead towards the road. Shortly after we saw more soldiers running and they stopped and asked us if we had seen a soldier and then ran after him. Later we were told he had run away with all the pay but we never found out if he got caught.

At 15 you had to join something so I joined the Air Training Corps. That took up three nights a week and Sunday mornings. Our HQ was at St Bede's and we had a social club at Ashburton House. Michael May let us use the old chapel there. We had a small library, a table tennis table and we could use the billiard table in the house. We used to go swimming in Woking and I remember one occasion when Mr May towed us on our bikes behind his mother's Austin 7. Thank goodness there was almost no traffic but Sergeant Lemon still stopped us and we all got told off, including Mr May. In the Air Training Corps we went to camp once or twice a year and we had a chance to fly. We also went to Vickers to get air experience, sometimes flying in new planes or newly repaired planes. They gave us a parachute but I don't know what would have happened if anything had gone wrong.

There was a lot of rivalry between Ripley boys and Send boys even before the war. On Wednesdays the Ripley boys came over to Send for woodwork. We often had fights and chased them back to the bus. Football matches between Send and Ripley were also very rough. We did not have any evacuees because we had two lodgers who worked at Secretts (Heath Farm). I had to cycle to Ripley to get the lodgers' rations. I used to go at 8 o'clock in the morning and then get out of Ripley quickly! There was also trouble with the evacuees, some of whom came from London and some from Portsmouth.

The Secrett family came from Ham, I think, and took over from Boormans either just before or just after the start of the war. Secretts was probably the biggest employer in Send and my dad worked for them during and after the war. Mr Secrett was a tough businessman. If he saw anyone smoking or not working hard enough he was known to have burnt a fiver in front of him or her and said that is what he or she had lost.

If he did not get the price he wanted for his veg then he would plough it in. If anyone tried to take any of it then they could be sacked or taken to court. I remember he rented an orchard over at Cobham and the apples were stored in a barn at Mays Corner, where the veg was washed. The trays of apples were piled up and he checked them regularly and the top trays were full, but when they were moved to go to market, the trays in the middle of the pile were empty! The houses on Send Road backed on to Secretts' land and on a foggy day several people sneaked out to cut cabbages. If they were concerned about the village policeman, who lived in one of the houses near Broomfields, they needn't have worried because he was already out in the field.

I don't remember going without (because of rationing). My mother had been in service and became a cook, so she made the most of what was available. Flour was short but she often used potatoes instead of flour. We had some chickens and when they went off lay they ended up in the pot.

On VE day I was at work, although I remember we went for a drink at the Jovial Sailor even though most of us were not old enough. I don't remember any other celebrations and because film was so scarce we did not have many photos as mementos.

At the end of the war I joined the Air Force aged 17 and a half. On VJ day I was at RAF Honiton, now Exeter Airport. We took part in a march through Exeter with Americans and French who were based locally. I spent two and a half years in the Air Force before going to Blackpool to get a new suit and being demobbed.

Sid Stanley (front second from right) with his fellow workers at May and Hardy.

MEMORIES FROM
PAT CLACK NÉE GIBBONS

My Dad did not drive, so when we thought we would like a day out we always hired Billy Challen from Send Garage. This was something of a mixed blessing because Bill couldn't see very well and I am sure, these days, would never have passed a driving test. However, my Dad's geography being excellent, he navigated Bill and we somehow always got there.

On September 3rd, 1939, we went down to Dorset to see my grandparents; Bill had taken us there before and always liked to go as he was treated as one of the family. Of course, the whole country was preparing for war, and when we arrived at 10.30 my Grandma said that Neville Chamberlain was going to speak at 11am She had a little battery radio and we all huddled round this and heard that we were at war.

At first things didn't seem to change very much – we had a few false alarms with air-raid warnings and food items began to be short; then of course we were issued with ration books and queues began to form for scarce items of food such as oranges, onions, etc. Very often we didn't know what we were queuing for we just joined a queue and hoped for the best!!! One thing I do remember was that Mrs Gus Sex – Gus was brother to Clarrie Sex who owned the forge – sold pies from her house every Thursday and Mum and I would go and buy from her. I think she had some sort of agreement whereby the pies were sold as a supplement to the meat ration, but you had to be there early as they were limited! She lived in Bush Lane.

I started work at Tyler's wine merchants in Chertsey Road, Woking, on leaving school, a month before war broke out.

WOOLTON PIE

Cooking time: about 1 hour   *Quantity:* 4 helpings

This pie is named after the Minister of Food—Lord Woolton. It is an adaptable recipe that you can change according to the ingredients you have available.

Dice and cook about 1 lb of each of the following in salted water: potatoes (you could use parsnips if topping the pie with mashed potatoes), cauliflower, swedes, carrots—you could add turnips too. Strain but keep ¾ pint of the vegetable water.
  Arrange the vegetables in a large pie dish or casserole. Add a little vegetable extract and about 1 oz rolled oats or oatmeal to the vegetable liquid. Cook until thickened and pour over the vegetables; add 3–4 chopped spring onions.
  Top with Potato Pastry or with mashed potatoes and a very little grated cheese and heat in the centre of a moderately hot oven until golden brown. Serve with brown gravy.
  This is at its best with tender young vegetables.

Listen to the Kitchen Front at 8.15 every morning

Dad wanted me to go to Clark's business school and do a shorthand/typing course, but I wanted to start work straight away, so attended Miss Duggan's typing school in Woking for evening courses instead. Our bus service was excellent in those days – the company was called the Blue Saloon. I went to Woking on the bus, came home at lunchtime – had about 20 minutes indoors (Mum always had lunch on the table) and returned, so did it all in an hour, and the buses never let me down. Dad likewise: he had an office in Duke Street, Woking, and the

the ATC and WJAC met there. I joined the WJAC at the onset – Women's Junior Air Corps; we were the female side of the Air Training Corps, and the senior members of the ATC taught us marching, Morse code, etc. This stood me in very good stead when I later joined the WAAF. One person who taught us was John Charman, who still lives on Send Hill. Our Commandant was Mrs Martin, who was a teacher and she later became Mrs Moore and they lived on Send Hill where Lance Rawes, a previous Headmaster, once lived.

Pat Clack (centre) in uniform, on leave in London.

When the LDV (Local Defence Volunteers) was formed, later to be called the Home Guard, my father and Mr Parvin, from Tyler's off-licence, were quite early in volunteering. The Home Guard consisted mainly of young boys, elderly gentlemen (my father) and men waiting to be called-up (Mr Parvin, who later joined the RAF). They met at the top of Send Hill and had a hut in the

bus drivers would wait for him at night if he happened to be a couple of minutes late; he had a season ticket with them.

St Bede's school had just been built but wasn't opened immediately. It was left in case it was needed as a hospital, but they did have evening classes there and

sandpit, where they met. They would parade round the village in pairs at night. I don't really know what they could have done in the case of invasion because, in Send at least, they possessed a couple of guns and no ammunition, but they were willing.

Send Home Guard outside the Drill Hall, now Lancaster Hall.

The nights when both my father and I paraded were a real pantomime – I hadn't got used to tying my tie and had to enlist Mum's help, and Dad (being very corpulent) had to sit three stairs up in order for Mum to tie his boots.

Meanwhile we now had evacuees – two little girls called Doreen and Christine Scholes. Their elder brother Geoffrey was billeted at Kingfield and he would cycle over to see them. Their father was in the RAF and their mother in the NAAFI (Navy, Army and Air Force Institution). Their home was at Thornton Heath near Croydon, and the school amalgamated with Send School. I recall the animosity between Miss Perrin (Send's

headmistress) and one of their teachers, Miss Barber. Daggers drawn!!! Very different ideas. Because of the large numbers, school now had to be divided between the old building which was Send primary school, the Church Room and the Red Cross hut. Pupils would carry chairs on their heads to the latter and we would see the crocodiles going to and from lessons. When Miss Perrin's and Miss Barber's contingents were changing over, they would walk on opposite sides of the road!!

Our little girls were quite nervous, the younger one, Doreen, especially so, because of the bombing they had already experienced. They also arrived in a terrible state – vests, black stockings etc practically threadbare. Mum used some of our coupons to replenish their clothes.

I was very sorry for them when they arrived – they were all taken to the Drill Hall (now Lancaster Hall) and paraded on the stage, and local mums could choose the ones they wanted. So the prettiest or more engaging-looking ones went first and the others were left standing, with their gas masks in cardboard cases hanging round their necks. A bit like a slave-market really, especially when you think they had just left their homes and their mums. We had Christine for 18 months until she gained a scholarship and was moved on to Bracknell, and Doreen for a further year.

Despite the fact that we were receiving evacuees – a so-called safe area – we did see some bombing locally. The biggest one was just behind our house and it demolished two whole council houses – a miracle that no one was killed. They were the homes of the Greens and Strudwicks who were large families. Rose Green was lying on a horsehair sofa and the blast ripped off all her clothes and she was scratched by the pins from the sofa. Her sister Millie later developed meningitis and lost her hearing; they were re-housed over what is now Paul Weller's hairdressers and sawdust was put down in the road outside to deaden traffic noises. Millie

later attended the deaf school at Margate and she still lives in Wharf Lane. That night Doreen and Christine were just

Doreen Scholes with Pat and her mother.

about to say goodnight and go upstairs when we heard this terrific WHOOSH... We didn't hear the bang, which signified the bomb was pretty close. Dad and I left Mum to cope with the girls and we went out, only to find this great gaping hole where the houses had been.

We all went to bed that night a bit shaken, but in the blackout, of course, so it wasn't until the next morning that we discovered that the front bedroom ceiling was hanging down at a rather precarious angle and our lavatory pan had split, sending all the water on to Mum's best suite in the room below. We did receive War Damage but not until years later and it wasn't much!

Speaking of the blackout, we had a rather officious ARP (Air Raid Precautions) warden– a bit like Bill Pertwee in Dad's Army – and one night he knocked at our door and told Dad a light was showing. Dad prided himself on his blackout and said he didn't see how it could be, but when he persevered with the complaint, it transpired that he could see a small light underneath the door. So Dad said to him that he "didn't know the buggers were coming on their hands and knees!" Naughty!

The Home Guard held dances in the Drill Hall to collect funds for the War Effort – Dad was secretary and sent the money to Mrs Churchill; he always received a hand-written reply from her. The local girls would come in droves because the Army was based on the Broadmead, and the local mums would ask Dad to keep an eye on them, and not allow the girls outside with the soldiers! A difficult task! At least two of the Canadians came back and married local girls – Rob Lowe who married Jean Burns from Holly Cottage, Mays Corner, and Wally Wallace who married Sylvia Darling. They had to go home first for de-mob.

The Broadmead, of course, has always been damp and eventually the Army decided it was unfit for the soldiers, so they were moved out and, what do you know, the ATS (Auxiliary Territorial Service women) were moved in! Dad was also First Aid Corporal, the reason being that the young boys complained because Dad couldn't keep up with them owing to his corpulent tummy, when crawling under barbed wire, so they thought he was of more use back at base. Dad and I were both doing first aid courses at the same time, and used to practise on Mum. One night someone came to the door and she answered it with her head swathed in bandages and her arm in a sling, frightening the life out of the caller.

Mr Gibbons, in uniform, outside his home.

Later in the war we had Italian prisoners-of-war based at Jim Oliver's Send Court Farm – two of these married local sisters – the men were Michael Stefania and ? Mastromarco. I can't remember the sisters' maiden names but one is now back living in Send.

Canadians on the Rec.

One weekend the Canadians currently stationed here, put on a baseball match on the recreation ground against the locals. Two weeks later they were moved out and we heard most of them had been killed when their ship was bombed. Some of us in WJAC uniform went round with collecting-tins for the Spitfire collection. Metal such as old saucepans, etc., was also collected for this effort.

There were other local bombs – I was home for lunch from Tyler's one day when there was a dog-fight going on overhead and we had heard a series of loud bangs. "Dog-fights" were our boys against the Luftwaffe fighting overhead – we all, including children, used to go out and watch these spectacles, never thinking we were in any danger. This occasion was when Vickers was bombed and hundreds killed; it was given out that there were "light casualties", but I had two uncles and an aunt working there and one was on first aid duty, so we heard the truth from him. It was said that some of the German boys had been over here prior to the War and knew the layout of the factory.

We also had at least two V-bombs (doodlebugs) fall, one halfway up towards Burnt Common, when a young man was killed walking down, and another when a cottage was destroyed at Burnt Common and a father, mother and two girls aged 16 and 3 were all killed. This was the Privett family; there is a plaque in Send Church to them. Their brother was at the time cycling home to his lunch and that was what he found on his arrival.

I wasn't here for the commencement of the V bombs – I had by this time joined the WAAF (Women's Auxiliary Air Force). I left home on March 8th, 1944, and didn't come back for leave until August, because there was a leave ban on. I wasn't home legitimately then – I was by this time at Compton Bassett on a wireless operator course, and some of us decided to put bolsters in our beds, (to simulate bodies for inspection) and try and get home. We "hitched" in those days, mostly getting picked up in batches by lorries, and I got a very good hitch from the Malmesbury Road into Guildford, but the main trains had gone, so I got a train as far as Clandon and walked from there, arriving very late at night. On my way down Burnt Common I heard this peculiar noise behind me – it made the hairs stand up on the back of my neck! – and I remembered what Mum and Dad had told me about these machines. When they cut out you knew they were about to fall – this one did, and I think it fell towards Horsley.

I got home and couldn't make anybody hear so threw some pebbles up to their bedroom window; they were horrified when they knew I had walked from Clandon at that time of night. I used Clandon quite a lot after that, because there was very seldom any porter on duty, and if you could get on at one end with a platform ticket you didn't need one the other end (I hope I haven't passed any of these tricks on to my children!). Another WAAF friend lived at Horsley too, and she would run across the fields to the train to join me. I had a friend, also in the WAAF, who still lives at Kingfield and when we were stationed at Bush House we obtained living-out passes, which meant we came home some nights. There was always a mad dash when we were on late turn, to get off the train and catch the last bus, which was about ll.30-midnight, and always packed with passengers standing all down the middle. The drivers soon got used to waiting for us and always packed us in regardless. When on early turn I would walk from home to Woking station at 5a.m. and sometimes get picked up by Mr Strudwick driving a Post Office van – this was also illegal!!!

While in the WJAC, we had socials combined with the ATC at St Bede's school, and these were always successful. We had quite a wealth of talent including the Burt twins – Sim and Tim – from West Byfleet, who did wonderful impersonations of the Western brothers and sang current songs, and Dennis Chinnery who still lives, I believe, in Horsell; he did a marvellous interpretation of a bombing raid; the lights were put out and simulated searchlights were on the ceiling – he did ALL the sounds, bomber crews talking to each other, aircraft noises, etc. (These three appeared on the first performance of a show called "First Flights" on the radio, which was ATC talent discovered from all over the country.) In our group we had Dorothy Knight – still in Woking – a good tap-dancer and others, but I had no talent so usually made the tea or sold programmes!! While I was in the WAAF, if my leave coincided with Armistice Day, I took part in what was then a big parade, including Melly Sanger, Irene Hobbs (WAAF) and several men – Jack Lepper (Army), George Masters (Navy) etc.

Mrs Sanger (who was a leading light in the WVS (Women's Voluntary Service) was always first on the spot when there was anybody in trouble - and particularly when a bomb fell at the top of Send Hill - with soup, blankets etc.

Mum used to save up sugar and other rations so that the evacuees could have good birthday parties here, and on my WAAF friend's 21st birthday (as she was Welsh and couldn't get home) she did a small party here for her too.

CHOCOLATE BISCUITS

Melt 2 oz margarine and 1 tablespoon warmed syrup. Mix in 1 oz Bournville cocoa, 4 oz flour, 2 oz sugar, ¼ teaspoon bicarbonate of soda and 1 teaspoon vanilla essence. Beat well, roll out cut into squares, place on a baking sheet and prick. Bake in a moderate oven about 15 minutes. Sandwiched together with chocolate spread page 85.

TEA-TIME FANCIES

2 oz fat
2 oz sugar
1 level tablespoon Bournville cocoa
1 dried egg, reconstituted

4 oz self-raising flour
1 level teaspoon baking powder
pinch of salt
about 2 tablespoons milk

METHOD: Cream fat and sugar, add cocoa and beat in the egg. Sift together flour, baking powder and salt and stir into the mixture alternately with a little of the milk until the consistency is soft and creamy. Put a spoonful of the mixture into greased and floured patty pans and bake about 20 minutes in a moderate oven. When cold slice off the tops, spread liberally with Mock Cream page 61 and replace tilted to show the filling.

CHOCOLATE FLAVOURING

All the family will enjoy cakes and biscuits given a chocolate flavour, this is easily achieved as you will see from the recipes on the various pages.

MEMORIES OF

Doreen Scholes - Evacuee

I lived with the Gibbons family from September 1940 until July 1942. My sister Christine was there only one year as at 11+ she moved to her grammar school near Bracknell. The only local child I knew well was Peter Parvin, who lived in the off-licence at the corner of the road. He was bigger but much younger than me. My most painful memory, literally, was being bitten by an Airedale dog, which Peter had been teasing, and then having to show Peter the bite on my bottom!

Other than that incident, I remember Mrs Gibbons was very kind to us. School life was good – I was successful. By this time we were used to rationing but we never went hungry. But having to say goodbye to our parents after visits left the most lasting scars. I found it difficult to say goodbye for many years, until I realised why this was so.

Doreen and Christine Scholes.

MEMORIES OF

SYLVIA WALLACE NÉE DARLING

IN PARTICULAR AN UNFORGETTABLE VE DAY

I was 12 at the outbreak of World War 2 and living at Mays Corner with my mother and older brother. He joined the Air Force and hoped to be a navigator but they discovered he was colour blind so he could not fly, which pleased my mother. I joined the Women's Junior Air Corps and we had weekly meetings at St Bede's.

I was at the school on Send Hill and I can remember on one occasion my friend and I were walking to school when enemy fighter bombers came low over the trees, pursued by a lone Spitfire. There was a group of five and six year olds, also going to school, who were screaming with terror and we shepherded them into the shelter of the bank at the side of the road until the danger was passed. When we got to school we were told off for being late! About 20 minutes later a local man came to the school and the teacher asked the two girls who were late to stand up and I thought we were in more trouble but he had come to commend us for our action.

On another occasion I was class monitor and was returning from the big tin hut in the school grounds, where I had been to check that the room was ready for girls' cookery, when a dogfight broke out overhead. A stray bullet hit the wall next to me and I ran into the school where I was met by the teacher, arms folded, who told me off for running!

We had no shelters at the school and if the siren went we sat in the cloakroom. There were a lot of glass windows around this room and the older pupils had to hang their coats up to minimise the danger of flying glass.

A lot of bombs fell in and around Send. The one that fell at Mays Corner was the biggest in Surrey up to that point; it was a thousand pound bomb. We were outside watching a silver plane with searchlights on when we heard a swishing sound. We had been told that if it were a whistling sound then it would fall several miles away but if it was a swishing sound then we should run for cover. My sister had opened the door for me to get in and the blast went through our house and I was thrown through the air. Two houses were destroyed and the crater took up the whole of both gardens but amazingly no one was killed. There were four men playing cards in the window of one of the houses and you could not see their faces for blood from the flying pieces of glass but my mother cleaned them up. After the blast a wardrobe was propping up the roof of one of the houses and as it was a windy night, it made a lot of banging and some people actually complained about the noise.

Another incident occurred when a bomber was being shot at by the guns on the Broadmead and the pilot must have decided to drop all his bombs. One fell where Send Close now is, another on the Rec and one in the sandpit but amazingly they all missed the road and the houses. I also remember the doodlebug coming down at Burnt Common, when most of one family was killed. I was ill in bed at the time and I heard it coming and told the nurse, 'here comes one of those flying things' but she couldn't believe I could hear it from that distance. Sadly the family had just switched from day work to night work, so they were all home in bed. There were two little boys from the family at school who survived and one 14 year old who was cycling home at the time it happened.

In the big house in Send Barns Lane, opposite what is now the new surgery, there were offices during the war and there was a girl from Wales working there. It was very quiet in Wales; you would hardly have known there was a war on. Her boyfriend came to visit her and a doodlebug hit the top of some trees, near where he was walking. He was killed by the blast but he looked as if he was asleep.

As a teenager I was allowed to go to a dance once a week in the village hall. There were soldiers manning the guns on the Broadmead and living in huts by the edge of the road but the off-duty soldiers were allowed to come to the dances. Prior to D-Day there were Canadians stationed in Send, the 85th and 86th Bridge Building Units, and they lived under canvas in a big field where Send Close now is. They were here to practise bridge building on the local ponds. They played baseball on the Rec and organised picture shows and dances in the Drill Hall (Lancaster Hall). They had a little shop at the Drill Hall and I sometimes think my mother let me go to the dances because I could buy chocolate bars there. I remember they had an ugly cook who wore a purple T-shirt with an orange dragon on it. He used to make things like rice pudding and the local children would queue up for him to feed them. Most of the Canadians were killed after leaving Send, I think. There was a quiet black man, called Bill, a schoolteacher, who was left with just one arm and no legs. Another young boy, called Peter Nicoli, who had lied about his age to get in the services, and whom all the mothers liked, did not make it.

During the war the main shops in Send were Mays Stores, next to Pat Clack's, which was a general store run by Miss May and Mrs Lee, the Post Office and the Co-op (now the funeral directors) and Webb's Store at the bottom of Potters Lane, run by Mr Lemon. We did most of our shopping at Mays Stores. I do not remember going without too much. I was lucky as after leaving school I worked in a parachute factory in Woking and I got a cooked meal there each day and was sometimes able to bring things home.

By VE day I was nearly 18 years old and my friend and I went to Woking but it was dead so we decided to get on a train to Guildford. We ran and jumped on the train, not realising the train divided and we ended up at Aldershot. We had to wait for the train to Guildford but as Aldershot was dirty and horrible we went back to the station. A serviceman stuck his head out of the train and I asked him if it was the right train, which it was. He was a Canadian, travelling with his French Canadian friend and we exchanged a few words on the train but not a real conversation. I knew my mother did not approve of girls going out with Canadians. In Guildford my friend and I got a bus back to Send and the two Canadians got on as well but when we got off at Mays Corner they stayed on the bus. However, later that day they appeared at the dance in Send and he, 'Wally', walked me home to Mays Corner. I told my mother about him but I never expected to see him again.

The following Friday, much to my surprise, when I got off the bus from Woking, the Canadian got off the Guildford bus and I took him back to meet my mother. He told her he had a 48-hour pass and nowhere to stay. My mother asked him to stay with us and they got on really well. Eventually he returned to Canada and we wrote a lot

Bill Darling with his wife Esme and baby Bruce together with Sylvia, 'Wally' and baby Marilyn.

and I tried to get out there. He sent me an engagement ring to help my chances of being allowed into Canada but to no avail. He decided to come to England but it was 13 months before he came back. We were married on 8th March 1947 and decided to settle here.

MEMORIES OF
MRS STEVENS NÉE TOGHILL

Mrs Stevens, who was born in 1911, and her daughter Jennifer (b.1951) said that the Stevens family have been in Send for about 400 years. Her husband, Ernest 'Steve' Stevens, was born on 10th January 1921 at 101 Send Road. Before the war Ern, as he was then known, was employed in the print room at Unwins where he worked a 51½ hour week for 9s 6d (47½p) but he really wanted to be a blacksmith. When war broke out he joined the Army and his younger sister Jessie did war work at Kenwoods in Old Woking. Ern, now known in the army as Steve, saw action in North Africa and was injured near Cairo. He was taken by air to a hospital near Johannesburg and finally returned to recuperate in Liverpool.

When he was fit he became an army driver based at Worplesdon where he met his future wife. Mrs Stevens, née Toghill, was stationed in Aldershot and in the ATS as a driver. Driving jobs included driving ambulances, POWs and officers. On one occasion she was driving an entertainment officer called Henderson to a show and he offered to get her a seat. Meanwhile she helped a

Send Church

fellow driver, Steve, to back his lorry and Henderson then said 'I suppose you will want two seats now'! The relationship developed from there.

On a short leave in 1945 Steve proposed in the front room at 101 Send Road and she accepted. They were married by special licence and had to queue up in London to get it and managed to jump ahead of another couple as they were getting married sooner. They were married at Send church on 18th July 1945 and unfortunately homemade buttonholes were forgotten, perhaps deliberately! They had their wedding breakfast in London.

Steve was still in uniform and managed to come home for a visit using an army truck, which he hid in Sandy Lane. They lived for a while in Taunton, where Steve was still in army barracks but after he was demobbed they lived in Tadwick, his mother-in-law's home. He took a course in stonemasonry in Bristol and worked, with others, on a variety of projects, notably Bath Abbey, where there is a plaque to recognise their craftsmanship. In 1957 the family moved to Australia where there was plenty of restoration work. Steve's father died on Boxing Day 1963 and in 1970 Jennifer Stevens, their daughter, returned from Australia and lived with her grandmother and Aunt Jessie in Send. After briefly returning to Australia she came back in 1974, met her future husband and was married, like her parents, in Send Church in 1975.

Her parents returned to live in England in 1977 and her father worked on the ranges at Bisley. He died in January 2004 at the age of 83. His widow lives in Old Woking and is 94 years old. (Memory recorded in 2005)

MORE BOMBS FALL IN SOUTH

COUNCIL HOUSES HIT

MANY CASUALTIES: SOME FATAL

When a flying bomb fell on a group of Council houses in the South of England on Monday four people were killed and several injured.

Of the group of houses some were completely demolished and the others were badly damaged. Other houses and premises in the district were also damaged by blast. These included several greenhouses, belonging to a nurseryman.

Another bomb, which fell on the same day a few miles away, landed on the green of a small village. Very little damage from blast was caused.

A parish church hall a men's club, and a Baptist chapel were among buildings damaged on Monday by a flying bomb which fell in a Southern England district. There were no fatal casualties, but some people were hurt.

Four adults and a child were in an Anderson shelter when the bomb fell on allotments only about ten yards away, but they all escaped unhurt, with the exception of a slight injury to a foot of a girl.

A woman who was in the shelter said to a reporter, "I was on a visit from North London to my sister, Mrs. How. Fortunately, the entrance to the shelter was on the side opposite to the place where the bomb exploded, so the blast did not get to us."

Pointing to the ruins of his hall, the vicar of the parish said, "For seven years I have been trying to raise the money to pay the debt on the building."

MEMORIES OF

GILBERT PRIVETT

Gilbert Privett was born in East Clandon on 28th September 1928 and he and his family moved to Burnt Common in the mid 1930s. He attended school in Send and was one of the first intake into St Bede's. In 1942 he left school aged 14 and went to work at Gibbs, who made agricultural machinery in Ripley. This was a relatively new enterprise in Ripley as it had been set up in 1939. Gilbert started as a trainee fitter and eventually rose to be a senior fitter. On 21st August 1944 Gilbert was cycling home for lunch. He walked as far as Grandis Cottages with a girl who worked in the leatherworks opposite Gibbs and whom he knew from school days. There was no roundabout at Burnt Common in those days but a crossroads, with Fogwills nursery on one corner, a corrugated building, garage and café on another corner. As Gilbert turned the corner towards his home, he heard a voice shout, 'In the ditch!' and he and the insurance collector, who had shouted, jumped in the ditch. Gilbert remembers there was an almighty explosion and by the time the dust settled there was just a pile of bricks. There were eight cottages at Burnt Common, of which two had been demolished by a doodlebug. The other cottages had broken windows and blast damage.

Gilbert was the first one on the scene. He remembers climbing over the rubble looking for his family and he had to be taken off by the ARP warden or some other member of the voluntary services. Mr Purser, his 'governor' from Gibbs, was also there shortly after the doodlebug fell. Gilbert lost his father and mother, his older sister Violet and his youngest sister Joyce in the explosion. His father worked at the former tannery at the Crack Processing plant for Mr Hamburger and had come home for lunch. His sister Violet, aged 21 worked at Connaughts, then Pantiles, on night work, where they did repairs for Fairoaks at Chobham and she was therefore at home asleep. His sister Joyce was too young to be at school but his two younger brothers and a sister were safe, as they had had lunch at school.

The remaining children were left with nothing and Gilbert learnt later that as orphans they might have been shipped off abroad. Luckily they had relatives locally and Gilbert went to live with his aunt and uncle, Mr and Mrs Bowers in Send. He told us how much he admired his uncle who had lost a leg in North Africa but, despite his artificial leg, he managed to cycle to work in Horsell and even to referee football on the Rec. Sister Yvonne went to live with an aunt and uncle at Liss and the two boys, Gordon and Derek, went to members of the family at Addlestone. Sadly he lost his brother Derek to diphtheria a year later. He said his sister Yvonne eventually married and went to live in Birmingham, living in Wolverhampton in her retirement. When she died her husband said she wished to be buried with her parents. The original grave had not been marked and so the vicar of Send had to hunt out the record books and eventually they pinpointed the grave. His sister's ashes were laid to rest in Send churchyard and the family also added a memorial stone to mark the grave.

Returning to 1944, Gilbert recalled that he found it hard to grieve and immersed himself in work. As well as working at Gibbs, he attended Woking Technical College two nights a week. He and the other fitters had to cycle out to jobs, some as far as the Hog's Back. (He eventually worked for Gibbs for over 48 years and was disappointed not to reach 50 years before the Ripley works were closed.) In 1946 he was conscripted into the Forces and, although the war had ended, he said his first thoughts were that he could not get in the Forces fast enough. He joined the RAF but was not given an engineering job, as would have seemed logical, but as he put it, 'it was peculiar how things turned out' since he was sent to RAF Henlow to guard German POWs. He said he found it hard to settle and he could not find out why he had been given this particular task especially as it was known he had lost his family in the war. Later the station adjutant said they knew he would not stand any nonsense from the prisoners. He agreed that initially he had felt angry towards the Germans but

later he accepted that most of them were only doing what they were told. The Germans were eventually repatriated and he moved on to other duties before returning to Gibbs.

He said the loss of his family was something he could not talk about for many years but things gradually got better and he feels over the years he has mellowed. This was perhaps demonstrated by recently encountering one of the Wright twins, who had survived the blast in a Morrison shelter in the adjoining cottage to his. He said they hugged each other and were able to talk about the events of that terrible day in 1944.

On a lighter note, Mr Privett recalled that military convoys rumbled through Ripley night after night and because of the blackout and the deflectors on the headlights they often hit the bridge at Bridge Foot. This was forever being repaired and sometimes vehicles ended up in the stream.

Memorial in Send Church.

MEMORIES OF

FRED DIXON

TAKEN FROM HIS MEMOIRS, 'THE STRAIGHT FURROW'

In the summer of 1939, we were spending our summer holiday at Paignton, when a telegram recalled me to Ripley. On Sunday, September 3rd, war was declared on Germany, and the evacuation of children from our cities to the countryside began. Ripley Court School – Captain Pearce, staff and pupils – was evacuated to Wales. There Captain Pearce died and his body was returned to Ripley where he was buried in the family vault.

Ripley was chosen to receive children first from Fulham and then from Portsmouth. The school was used as a reception and medical inspection centre. Every child carried a bundle or case, and a square cardboard box

Evacuee children (not taken locally).

containing a gas mask. A label with their name and address was attached to their clothes.

With two hundred and twenty children at school, our resources were strained to the utmost and eventually we had to overflow into the church hall, which was already in use for thirty difficult girls from Ryde House hostel. On certain afternoons the hall was used by church organisations and the children had to be accommodated in the main school building- three in a desk built for two.

One evening, at about 10.00 p.m. during the blackout, old Mr Stanbridge, who lived in West End cottages, came to my door. He told me that he was having trouble with his three Fulham evacuee boys, aged 5, 9 and 13. They had arrived in Ripley only the previous day and were billeted with him just off the main road. It seems that the Browning boys were homesick. Poor lads, I could sympathise with them. City life and village existence were so different, and running by their front door every twenty minutes

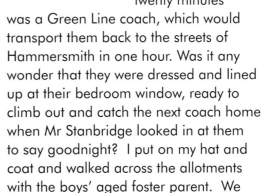

was a Green Line coach, which would transport them back to the streets of Hammersmith in one hour. Was it any wonder that they were dressed and lined up at their bedroom window, ready to climb out and catch the next coach home when Mr Stanbridge looked in at them to say goodnight? I put on my hat and coat and walked across the allotments with the boys' aged foster parent. We all sat at a table, three boys, Mr and Mrs Stanbridge and myself. I told the boys that first thing tomorrow I would send a telegram to their father and ask him to come down as soon as he could so long as they promised not to do anything silly like running away. Their father came down immediately and his visit sorted things out. The Browning boys settled down better than most of the evacuees and were among the last ones to leave the district for home.

Another evacuee family had a problem father in London. The two boys and a girl found shelter with

Fred Dixon, Headmaster of Ripley School.

my assistant gardener, Stephen Bradley and his wife, who lived in Newark Lane. Mrs Bradley drew my attention to the state of the elder boy's boots. There was very little sole left and, in one place on each foot, he was walking on his socks. The reception committee had by this time dispersed, so Mrs Bradley had written to the father who was a clerk in the Ministry of Supply. She received no reply, so as the wet autumn was well advanced she came to me. The need was urgent so I telephoned the Secretary of the Guildford RDC who said, "I can do nothing for a week, Mr Dixon, as my

Committee does not meet before then". I suggested that red tape should be cut and boots purchased at once. I told him that I would go to a local shoe shop, buy the boy a pair of boots and send the bill to the RDC for presentation to the committee when next they met. He said, "Yes, do that Mr Dixon, but pay for them and send me the receipted bill". Even in wartime, officialdom was so tied with red tape that there seemed no way of refunding the cost of the boots either from the father direct, or through some account. In order to reimburse me, a London County Council's Children's Christmas Party Fund was raided by a local organiser.

In almost every case the people of Ripley received the evacuated children with open arms, but the one exception was prevented from doing so by something, which stood for religion. One Sunday, a number of evacuees arrived from Worthing. This evacuation was a sudden decision on the part of the Government because of the imminent possibility of invasion. Ripley was totally unprepared for it and the only available member of the reception committee was Mr Tom Goodman, the Clerk to the Parish Council. It was obvious that he could not cope on his own so I contacted Mr Brind, the Portsmouth evacuee teacher, and the two of us took over reception duties about 11.00 am. There was to be no church for us that day. We worked at registration throughout the day while Tom Goodman toured the area trying to find billets. When my wife and Mrs Brind came out of church at 8.00 pm we only had to find places for one woman helper and her two grandchildren. We had gone through the village with a fine-tooth comb and then I suddenly remembered an elderly widower living alone in a four-bedroomed house. He had not been on our list because we could not have expected him to look after even one child, let alone a family. But this was a different proposition- a widow who would do everything for her two grandchildren in the accommodation provided.

I personally called on him and presented our case. "No, Mr Dixon", he said with a sob in his voice and tears in his eyes, "I am on good terms with them up there" – pointing heavenward- "and I do not wish to disturb the relationship". "But even Christians must eat and sleep on Sunday" I said and I quoted, "In as much as ye did it unto the least of these, ye did it unto me". "No, no, Mr Dixon", he said "Not today. Come and see me tomorrow". "It will be too late then. Sleep well", I said as we parted. I never gave him a second chance as we managed to fit the evacuees in with a person who needed a housekeeper. I

was surprised that the Vicar adopted the same attitude. He said that it was wrong on the part of the authorities to evacuate the south coast on Sunday. I told him that as an ex-serviceman with the rank of Major, he should realise that nations at war do not recognise the Sabbath.

It was obvious to some people in the village that when war was declared bombs would drop on and around the

Ripley School.

village. We were only three and a half miles, as the bomber flies, from the Vickers aeroplane factory (later British Aerospace) at Weybridge. In fact the intensity of bombing at Ripley proved to be greater than that in Guildford or Woking.

Air raid shelters were being built for schools in the Cobham, Woking and Guildford areas, but the villages nearest Vickers received no such attention.

Parents in Ripley were indignant and two or three leading villagers decided that if the authorities would not provide shelters for the children, they would. I reported to the Chief Education Officer that the people in the village were determined to have shelters. The next day the Chief HMI, Mr Heath, said, "The idea is ridiculous. The Germans will not come over between the hours of nine and four, and somebody ought to tell the people so". I retorted that I would certainly not prophesy what the Germans would do. He said, "Well, would you come over in daylight?" and I replied that if I were in the German Air Force and were commanded to come, I would have to whether I wanted to or not.

I then asked the County Architect if he would supply me with particulars relating to the Surrey County Council's requirements for the construction of shelters and he replied "No". I then asked him if he would view some block plans for approval if I submitted them to him. He replied, "Yes". He only spoke those two words throughout the interview. The block plans were produced by a member of a concrete construction company, whose works were near the village, and I forwarded them to the County Architect. They were returned with his approval accompanied by a letter saying that the Surrey County Council would accept no liability or responsibility for them in any way.

The Vicar was quite opposed to the shelter scheme. Before we were allowed to put an excavator to work in the playground I had to sign a statement that I would reinstate the playground when the war was over. The Vicar urged me not to have anything to do with the project in case it affected my career. I

Reverend M Evan Thomas shown here with pre-war school group.

had no doubt at all that what I intended to do was the right thing.

Concerts, whist drives, jumble sales, dances etc. now engaged our attention. As the money became available we bought pre-fabricated concrete sections. Cement, sand and labour were all given and machinery was loaned. Mr Barrett, the portable building manufacturer on the Portsmouth Road, made a generous gift of seating for 200 children to use in the shelters. As yet we had no money for heating, lighting or ventilation. When completed, we had four shelters each capable of holding up to fifty children, and at one time we managed to pack a total of two hundred and fifty into them. They were amongst the best school shelters in Surrey.

When the shelters were almost completed, German planes bombed Vickers aircraft works at Weybridge in daylight and killed several workers who were just leaving the canteen. We had organised a garden fete on our tennis court at home for the shelter fund, and when the planes appeared almost overhead the tables and stalls were covered with white cloths and paper. The planes were very low and the black crosses were easily seen. It struck me that they would see our display of white cloths and look upon them as a sign of surrender. This would never do, so I hastily whipped them from the tables and stuffed them underneath.

The first intimation that they were enemy planes was when the anti-aircraft guns opened up on them. One bomber was brought down at Ockham and the wounded pilot was captured. He was brought to the doctor's surgery opposite the school for treatment but had to wait until Dr. Creet returned. The pilot had been wounded in the leg. Somebody managed to capture his flying boot complete with splinter holes and Fred Bushnell carried it around the village using it as a collecting box for our shelter fund. The local ARP group linked the school with the police station by means of a cable with a loud buzzer in Room 4. In this way we received immediate notice of all air-raid alerts. This room was later used for the Fire Watchers' nightly vigil in the centre of the village, and camp beds were installed for those resting.

All schools received a directive from County Hall that all windows in schools were to be faced on the inside with transparent material pasted to the glass to prevent shattering and consequent casualties if bombs dropped near. This order was repeated later, except that broad strips of brown gummed paper were to be fixed vertically and horizontally for the same purpose. Lucky were those heads of schools who had full-time male caretakers to put the order into effect. My part-time caretakers, both women, were unable to do it, and I had to carry out the work on my own.

One evening after school, two boys, John Hutson and a Portsmouth evacuee named Maurice Mercer, borrowed my wheelbarrow so that they could canvass their assigned area for salvage. Salvage thus collected was carted away, sorted, and used in the war effort. During the course of their perambulations the boys collected some glass soft drink bottles. They realised immediately that here was a grand opportunity to help themselves and the country at the same time by returning the bottles to a local shop at a penny or twopence a time. However duty called and they had to collect salvage, so they hurriedly hid the bottles in the hedge in Tom Gunner's garden, which fronted Newark Lane. I had been working on the allotments, but it was getting dusk as I walked home. I was barely indoors when the guns opened up, and this was followed a few moments later

John Hutson aged about 7 or 8

by a frantic banging on the knocker of our front door. I opened the door and John and Maurice nearly fell into my arms. "Can we come in, Mr Dixon?" said John. "Jerry's up!" I brought them in and pushed Joan, my daughter, John and Maurice into the knee-hole of my desk. Then the bombs began to fall. The second one dropped on the edge of the Green about a hundred yards from our house and blew the large key out of the back door. "Coo!" said a voice, "That's the best we've had yet!" It was how Maurice would have voiced his appreciation of a firework display.

The third bomb demolished a house where the occupants had gone out; the fourth smashed the front of Tom Gunner's cottage, but the Gunners were in the back room and they and their dog were unhurt; the fifth dropped in the yard of Legge's tea shop (the recently closed Town and Country Cars, on the corner of Newark Lane) and only left a hole in the concrete; bomb six dropped fair and square on the cross-roads. The Vicar was at the door of the Vicarage speaking to John's sister Irene when they both heard it coming. They fell to the ground and the Vicar gallantly covered Irene's body with his own; another bomb fell on the tennis court at Chapel Farm in Rose Lane and the others just dropped in open fields. The plane's run was from north to south.

When the dust had settled John and Maurice sallied forth to "finish the job". They went to the spot were they had left their bottles – nothing but broken glass met their gaze. The bomb, which smashed Tom Gunner's house, had upset their plans to enter the money market! Tom Gunner and his wife collected all their unbroken china and glassware and placed it carefully in their shed, which had not been damaged.

The next bombing of the village occurred later in the evening on a Saturday. On this occasion it was from east to west. Mr Shoesmith's house was demolished (later rebuilt as Nos. 98 and 99 High Street) and he and his wife, daughter and mother-in-law were all buried in the rubble but were unhurt except for a slight cut on old Mrs Carter's ear. On being rescued Mrs Carter's chief concern was for her handbag, which lay buried in the rubble! The second bomb dropped in an open space between a cluster of cottages on Greenside – the crater occupied almost the whole of the vacant area; the third bomb fell on Tom Gunner's shed containing all his salvaged glass and crockery and blew out the rear wall of a neighbouring cottage. A baker who had retired early for the night suddenly found himself still in bed at the bottom of a crater in the garden. The last bomb dropped on the allotments.

The following day – Sunday – Mr Chapman, a local butcher, and his friend Richard Bondy visited me after lunch. Mr Bondy did the talking: "Mr Dixon, I have a proposition to make to you. I will pay to ventilate, heat and light your shelters with electricity on one condition- that you allow the village people to use them out of school hours". This seemed too good to be true. Of course, there never had been any intention to exclude the adults from the shelters for they had provided the money for them and all the labour.

Some nights later, in the early hours of the morning, some 1500 incendiary bombs fell on and around the village.

Fortunately little damage was done but the scenic effect was beautiful. Tree and hedges were silhouetted in black against a background of white light and it was as if one had been transported to fairyland.

Many families evacuated from the Elephant and Castle area in London used the shelters, and when London was bombed the shelters were placed at the disposal of the people who had lost their homes. These unfortunate people were accommodated in the church hall; the women slept on the stage with drawn curtains, and the men slept on the fixed seats along the sides or on the floor. I went down two or three times and on the last occasion I took some old safety razors, blades and shaving soap which were in short supply, for the people had brought nothing with them. As I entered the hall an old lady said "Cor lumme Guv'nor, don't bring us anything more or you'll make us cry". We spent a total of seventy-six hours in the shelters – forty-two for ordinary daylight raids and thirty-four for the flying bombs or "doodlebugs", later known as V1s to distinguish them from the V2s which were rockets. These two weapons were calculated by Hitler to devastate southern England.

One day at about 11.00 a.m. a V1 was heard approaching the village followed by an explosion. The children were in the shelters but from my position in the playground I could see a plume of smoke rising and it was clear that it had fallen on Ripley Green.

It occurred to me that the children would be worried about the safety of their parents, so I went first to the infants' shelter. I need not have worried. As I descended the steps I heard the strains of "Jesus loves me this I know" coming from fifty childish throats. This was undoubtedly Miss Marsh's contribution to their morale. In the second shelter the children were completely calm and unruffled, and as I reached it I heard "Pack up your troubles in your old kit bag". How often had I heard that sung during the shelling in the First World War and at the time I never imagined that I would hear English boys and girls singing it under similar circumstances. In the last shelter where the eldest children were, I heard the refrain "Put that pistol down, babe, put that pistol down. Pistol packing Momma, put that pistol down". This popular wartime song evidently indicated what they thought about the war.

I was so impressed by the behaviour of the 5-11 year old children that I thought the parents should know and appreciate the work of the teachers who were mainly responsible for them, so I sent a few special lines to the Vicar for inclusion in the parish magazine. While the children were in the shelters the time was never wasted and the opportunity was taken to commit to memory prose and verse passages and multiplication tables.

One night a very funny incident occurred in the ranks of the Home Guard at an observation post in Polesden Lane, which had been constructed in a tree. During an alert, when German bombers were in the vicinity, the post was manned by one sentry, with a corporal and two men on the ground. Major Kay was on his rounds and when he arrived at the post there was a battle royal going on between the group on the ground and the sentry up the tree. Major Kay enquired the reason for this strange behaviour in the presence of the enemy and the two accounts went along these lines. The corporal said "Well sir, we was standing 'ere at the foot of the tree when suddenly old 'Aynes (the sentry) up there started buzzing things down at us, so we retaliated". Haynes' version was exactly opposite to this. He said, "I was up the tree, sir, and them blighters started chucking things up at me". The truth was that the ack-ack guns were firing at the planes and the splinters were falling round the group on the ground. They thought that old Haynes had suddenly gone mad and quickly reacted in the way he had described, much to his annoyance.

Mr Heath, the HMI, was visiting us when an alert came through the buzzer system. I wondered if he remembered telling me that the Germans would never come over between the hours of 9am and 4pm. Actually he was quite right, they sent their pilotless planes to bombard us instead! The warnings came as soon as they were reported flying towards the coast where some of them were shot down. They quickly covered the forty miles to Ripley. They were extremely noisy and when they passed overhead sounded like loose ironmongery.

By this time we were adept at getting into the shelters. When an alert came through, the classes were taken out to their respective shelters but instead of filing into them they remained on the surface. Blackboards and easels were erected and lessons carried on in the daylight and fresh air. Each class divided into two and when the clanking machinery was heard a whistle was blown and, at the word "DIVE", each group entered the shelter at a different entrance and the whole school would be underground in ten seconds.

At the conclusion of the war, I submitted a report to every parent and to all helpers in the erection of the shelters, including all known donors. I said that the one thing for which the war was fought was that there should be freedom from fear. Through the shelters this had been achieved for the children and their parents at a cost of sixpence (2½p) per child hour. From the financial point of view alone it was well worth it, but the value to village morale was incalculable. This can be proved by comparison with the village of Send, which had no school shelters. A V1 fell on some cottages at Burnt Common. Mr Gay, the headmaster of St Bede's Secondary School, closed his school at once and sent the children to their homes, including those who lived at Burnt Common. The head teacher of the Primary School followed suit. No child at Ripley School had relatives who were amongst the casualties, but two of the children lived in one of the nearby homes. The Governors and Managers of the two Send schools communicated with County Hall demanding shelters before they considered it safe to open the schools again. They were provided with open trenches as a substitute. This of course took time, and during that time our school remained open and attendance remained steady around the 90% mark.

At the conclusion of the war I received a visit from the Chief County Inspector, Mr Gunton. As he was leaving the school I drew his attention to the shelters and asked him if he knew their history. He told me that he had heard something about them, then turning to me he said, "I think they are a monument to you, Mr Dixon". I then told him about the piece of paper containing my signature and held by the Vicar, where I promised to reinstate the playground at the conclusion of hostilities. He immediately "blew up" and said that he had never come across such an instance where a person's sense of social service had been treated in such a shabby manner. He went back to Kingston, gave them a piece of his mind and I received a letter from the Chief Education Officer to the effect that the Surrey County Council had accepted responsibility for the shelters. (NB The shelters were among the last remaining in the county, fitting reminders of the war, until the school itself was demolished in 1982.)

MORE MEMORIES

In addition to the more recent interviews included in this book we have many memories that have been collected over the years and compiled by Jane Bartlett. From these we have been able to extract some stories and some factual information, which help to paint a picture of what life was like in Send and Ripley during the war. (Jane's collection of memories is in a file and can be consulted at Ripley Museum.)

MORE MEMORIES
FROM SEND

At the outbreak of war in 1939 Send was still a very rural community, where market gardening played a large part in village life. Food production became an important issue during the war but local market gardening does not seem to have benefited the village as much as one would have supposed. This seems to have been down to the personality of the principal employer, Mr Secrett. Sid Stanley, in his recollections, has suggested that Mr Secrett, who had taken over a lot of land from Boormans, was not well liked and would plough in surplus produce rather than share it with villagers. His view was reinforced by Peter Rixon, who told the Society he thought that Mr Secrett was a hypocrite as he made his men work on Sunday but they had to keep out of sight when he and his wife went to the chapel for morning and evening service.

Florrie Bexley, née Brewer, also gave an interview to Jane Bartlett in 1989. She was born in 1902 and lived in Prews Farm for 73 years. She was born

there and continued to live there with her brother after her parents' death, until it was sold following Mr Secrett's death. She looked after her brother, who worked at Secrett's, mainly growing tomatoes. Sometimes Mr Secrett expected

".. every available piece of land must be cultivated

GROW YOUR OWN FOOD
supply your own cookhouse

her brother to get up at 2am to get things, such as new carrots, to market, and he took them on a lorry with Dick Whitton. She used to wake her brother as she had an alarm clock. One day she overslept and Mr Secrett came over and "did he tell me off" so I told him that I didn't get paid to get up at two in the morning!

She also remembered they had oil lamps and she recalled a bomb coming down at the little bridge just behind the sheds on the footpath and all the oil lamps swung. It was one of her jobs to fill and trim the paraffin lamps and they had tiny little oil lamps to go to bed.

Reg and Albie Giles who lived at Waters Edge, Potters Lane, told the Society of another local market gardener, Spooner, who had all the land behind Vision Engineering and up to Potters Lane. He had rhubarb in what is now the lake

area behind Reg's house, but later sold the gravel creating a pit behind the house. At first this was dug by hand by Jack Pullen until it reached six feet deep, then the dredgers came in. During the war there were Canadians based locally and they made a ramp at the far end of the lake, which has now grown over, where they slid down DUKW amphibious vehicles, to test their waterproof quality. The lake created by the pit was bigger then and took up half of Reg's plot, but later they had gravel and soil dumped in it to increase the size of his garden.

As well as cultivated fields, there was another open space in Send, the Broadmead. This was an area used for growing hay and grazing prior to the war, with an unusual medieval-style strip ownership. Margaret Bayliss of Potters Lane recalled what happened when war broke out. Her family owned a strip of the Broadmead but during the

Remnants of gun emplacements on the Broadmead

war the army commandeered it with no compensation. The army built gun sites and on the Baylisses' piece, built six huts for the men, with concrete footings, a concrete path to them and a concrete drive to the gun sites. They are still there today. After the war the gates to the Broadmead had gone with the army.

Many others both in Send and Ripley, including Winnie Upstone, recalled the sound of the heavy guns from the Broadmead. She also shared memories of the Canadians when, in 1988, she told the Society they tested tanks in the sandpits. She also remembered there were big guns on the Broadmead and, as well as a flying bomb at Send Barns Lane, there was a bomb at Mays Corner, at the end of her garden which seemed to lift her house up and down, and badly damaged the two houses at the bottom.

Bill Tickner also had memories of bombing in Send. During the 2nd World War a bomb fell in Tannery field, and a doodlebug on the big house, Major Trimmer's house, at Send Barns (now almost demolished). Bill was in the Home Guard, and the officer from Burnt Common ordered them to clear out the fallen plaster off the beds and clean up. A boy was killed walking up Send Road, but according to Bill no one took much notice. On another occasion Bill's brother was getting married before going into the Air Force, so Bill, then living at Cartbridge with his wife, cycled towards the stag party on a cold Friday night. He couldn't really hear the doodles "with the blooming wind". He heard screaming,

dived into a ditch, bike and all, and saw all the shrapnel sparks like stars. A stick of bombs fell across Luff's nursery (now Ripley Nurseries) leaving six holes.

Bob Whapshott also had memories of bombing, a flying bomb opposite what is now Kevan Drive. A chap was killed by it and Jim Oliver said, "No good sending for the ambulance, he's as dead as mutton." He said you got sort of hardened. Many recalled the bombing at Burnt Common when four people were killed. Bob was on his way home and saw pieces of debris going up and some chickens stuck in oak trees. The first two houses on the right hand side, had sides gone, the others lost glass. Dick Mellem's house collapsed afterwards. Dick's wife and Charlie Webber, the lodger, were inside but were sitting each side of the chimneypiece. He never got over it; she did, although both were injured. It was interesting that he said he had few recollections of Send as it was too far to walk and when he got down there, there were very few houses. Rather different to today.

Local defence in Send was provided not just by the regular forces but was supplemented by a local Home Guard, which met at the Drill Hall (now Lancaster Hall). Reg Tidy told us that during the war he joined the small fire brigade run by Gordon Stewart at the Manor. Irene Whiting, née Giles, was also able to add that she had worked at Stewart's Great Dane kennels for ten years and he had employed about 200 people. At its height there were about 500 dogs to exercise and feed. They had their own veterinary surgery and own bake-house for dog biscuits. However, when the war came he stopped breeding dogs and started a poultry farm, also pigeons, which were sent to Covent Garden for food – "squab pie". Fred Hookins also added to memories of Stewart's, recalling that the chicken farm was there until 1953 when the land was sold to Hall & Co.

Jane Bartlett interviewed Jean Anderson, of Send, in 1996, and she recalled the butcher's business her father ran in Send during the war. Her father, Henry Robert Pullen, was born in 1889 and worked as butcher and in the slaughterhouse at Old Woking, first with Tanner then with Smallridge, a butcher in Send Road. Mr Pullen set up on his own in business about 1938 in the outhouse by converting a laundry. He had a fascia signboard on the front of the drying room but people came down the side to what had been a washroom. There was a marble slab for cutting, a rail for the carcasses and he made a desk for paperwork and put lino on the floor. The meat came from Guildford and she thinks he had to pay a lump sum of £20

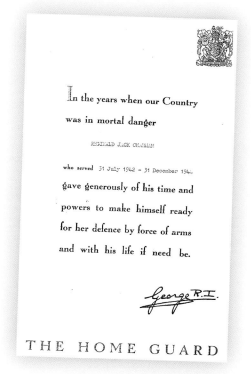

In the years when our Country was in mortal danger

REGINALD JACK CHARMAN

who served 31 July 1942 – 31 December 1944 gave generously of his time and powers to make himself ready for her defence by force of arms and with his life if need be.

George R.I.

THE HOME GUARD

in advance, which was a lot in those days and which he never got back.

In hot weather they had an icebox safe at the garden end of the store and ice was delivered twice a week. "Squibs" Kerwood, an ex-evacuee, was the one who delivered meat and probably told him about a spare ice chest when the American soldiers left the area.

Mr Pullen delivered on a trade bike with a basket on the front to Westfield, Sutton Green, Old Woking and even Clandon. Mrs Anderson knows that her sister sometimes delivered and also her brother Peter Pullen. Her father washed the place out on Wednesdays and on Saturday afternoons, scrubbing all the baskets on a table outside. He washed himself down in cold water outside in the yard every day winter and summer. He had a hand-turned sausage machine, as there was no electricity. He would tell visiting children, turn the handle and it will play a tune. Her father died in November 1945, but they were told not to close, as it was a vital food distribution place. The Ministry found a Polish man to help but he couldn't speak any English so George Smith was given exemption

Challens' garage, shown here post-war.

installed and war work was carried out for Vickers, Saunders Roe and Vokes. During the peak period work went on 24 hours a day with shift work carried out by local labour. Mike Sex told Sheila Brown that during the war the local forge was almost entirely employed with war work. He even lent a hand in the school holidays. He remembered parts being made for submarine hatches, MTB exhaust manifolds and bits for Bailey Bridges. In the forties there were as many as six forges going at one time as most farm work was still being done by horse and so the blacksmith was constantly employed.

from the army to carry on. The business seemed to be losing money after the War and her mother closed it in about 1950.

Another business in Send was Challen's Garage. Mrs Challen recalled that during the war they still had hand petrol pumps. The Army, who were stationed at Heath House, had sole use of the Shell pump. She also remembered that a workshop was built at the rear of the garage where four lathes and other machinery were

During the war Dick Lillywhite drove staff to Vickers and carried munitions to Vokes at Henley Park. He was then ordered to collect POWs from the camp on Merrow Downs and take them to all

Italian POWs working on a local farm.

the local farms, Germans and 'Eyties'. Apparently, the Germans did the main drainage system in Ripley. He tried to practise his schoolboy German on them but found they all spoke perfect English! John Hutson said that some of the Italian prisoners of war slept in the loft above Fauldes stables and worked on the farm. If they liked you they wove you willow baskets.

One of the most comprehensive accounts of wartime in Send came from Hope Sanger, who lived at Willingham Cottage in Farm Lane. Mrs Sanger was born in 1897 and gave a talk to the Send & Ripley History Society in 1988 on her role in the WRVS. The WRVS provided canteens for servicemen and war workers; they acted as drivers, organised food, clothing and shelter for evacuees and those made homeless. She was the Deputy Organiser for the Guildford Rural District and Marshal of the Rest Centre at the Drill Hall, which in 1942 became a shelter and depot for emergency food supplies. She was also billeting officer and had to rehouse the people made homeless by the bomb at Burnt Common in August 1944. When an unexploded doodlebug was detonated on Send Hill it caused substantial damage so she gave the Army a 'ticking off'.

Her recollection was that, in all, one hundred bombs dropped in Send. In particular she remembered the one that fell on the recreation ground at 9pm, one on Mrs Donn's house in Tannery Lane, and one on the Council estate.

Boughton Hall she said was used as a food store for evacuees (Ken French said it was also a hospital for infectious, sick evacuees). Twenty-two houses on Send Hill had roofs blown off and a doodlebug blew up in the sand pits. Tom Graham was a warden (presumably an Air Raid Warden) and the Red Cross took over the Church Room.

Mrs Sanger also remembered the bombing at Burnt Common when on 21st August 1944 four people were killed in the council cottages, Mr & Mrs Privett, a child and a visitor (actually a second child). She had a list of those injured and where people were put to stay, and what clothing was given out, e.g. Mr Miller went to Mr Nash, the Hollies, Burnt Common. Next door to Send Church there was a clothing store in the house belonging to Lady Boscawen. She also recalled Woolton Pies, which were a sort of vegetarian pasty and a supplement to rations. She and Mrs Gus Sex handed them out each week and took the names of those who received them.

During the War she drove for the Food Office delivering orange juice and issuing ration books. This gave her a good knowledge of the villagers and villages. Marjorie and Ron Sex were living in Guildford at that time, Michael May of Ashburton House was active in the village and Mrs Grantham lived in Aldertons. They were all on the Send Invasion Committee.

Landgirls in the snow

In 1942 the Send Invasion Committee had to consider a number of special measures, including alternative water supplies; tests showed The Tannery and Ashburton House to have the best quality water in the village. Other measures covered alternative sanitation, the treatment of casualties (severely wounded were to go to Boughton Hall, any overflow to Stewart's Manor House), the provision of a rest centre at the Drill Hall, food stocks and emergency lighting and heating. Volunteers to help with the Committee's tasks included Mrs Dockerty from The Tannery, Mrs Mellem of Oakhaven, Burnt Common, Mrs Thorpe from Elmsleigh, Send Barns, the Duchess of Westminster of Send Grove, Mrs Young from Pembroke House and Mrs Wilkins of Sendhurst Grange.

There was a volunteer car pool as they had to be able to get to hospital despite ice or snow. The volunteer Food Controller was Mr May from Ashburton House. There was a Billeting Officer who gave instructions for rehousing anyone who was bombed out and details re iron rations, transport and clothing. Send also had to cope with evacuees. They were scheduled to receive 60. The depot was at Boughton Hall, Send, under the supervision of Mrs Rickards. Each child was given a cotton bag of food that included corned beef, biscuits, condensed milk, compressed sugar, chocolate, tea and bread. There was also a clothing scheme and they had forms for writing to evacuee parents for clothes and coupons, also forms re money for mending evacuees' boots and shoes.

Home Guard gas mask drill

Bridie Strudwick, née Cavanagh, of Potters Lane said that during the war her husband was sent to Bath to work for the Admiralty. Arthur Sex, the Billeting Officer, was fixing up evacuees and brought her a family - Capt. Moore, wife and children - so she would not be lonely. They were relations of the doctor at Clandon. They stayed with her a long time and it was very nice.

Nancy Graham of 65 Send Road also had evacuees; two land girls, two women teachers and two children from South Shields. Arthur Sex also brought a family of five, all still bandaged up after being bombed out. They slept on mattresses on the floor until an empty cottage was found. Once Nancy had the art teacher from St Bede's to stay. Pat Clack's family also had evacuees lodging with them. Apparently Miss Evelyn Lancaster at Sendholme, had 11 evacuees, including a policeman's wife and 3 children, 3 German musicians and an Italian boy.

Peter Rixon remembered that during the war years they used the school buildings in the morning and then went to the Drill Hall in the afternoon, and the evacuees vice versa. In 1987 Miss Palmer, a teacher at Send School, confirmed these memories of the war years. She said that two evacuee schools arrived – Croydon pupils were in the church room and Putney pupils in the Drill Hall.

Later they amalgamated in the Drill Hall. Then they had a half-day in the school while Send School occupied the Drill Hall, alternate mornings and afternoons. For the first half of the session Infants and Lower Juniors had musical drill, games, story reading and occupations, followed by the Seniors. There was two weeks holiday duty in the summer for staff to allow evacuee staff a break.

SEND

WEDDING OF PILOT OFFICER HENRY AND MISS T. LASKIE

The wedding took place at Send Church on Saturday between Pilot Officer Ian Clifford Henry, only son of Mr. and Mrs. Clifford Henry, of Kinnord, Pyrford, and Miss Tania Laskie, elder daughter of Major and Mrs. S. F. Laskie, of Tinders, Cobham. The bride was given away by her father, and wore a silver dress with a long silver tulle veil and wreath of orange blossom. Her bouquet was of pale yellow roses and fern and she wore a diamond brooch, a gift from the bridegroom. She was attended by her sister, Miss Patricia Laskie, who wore a silver dress, with a head-dress of silver leaves, and carried a posy of yellow roses. Mr. Yainton Mills, Royal Tank Corps, was best man, and the groomsmen were Lieut. Gordon Rennie and Lieut. Richard Crichton, M.C. There was a reception at Three Fords, Send, the home of Mr. and Mrs. W. Russell Stokes. The honeymoon was spent in the New Forest, the bride travelling in a dusty-pink dress and matching hat, with veil, fur coat and grey accessories.

In 1941 the evacuees, with two members of staff, were amalgamated with Send Junior school allowing for a second class of infants. Sheila Brown has studied the Send School records and they revealed that at one point, due to staff shortages, Mr Penn was managing 80 children by himself. The school hours had to be shortened in winter to ensure the children could go home in daylight. In 1941 the schools were reorganised. The children over eleven went to St Bede's and Miss Perrin arrived as Head Teacher. She was born and educated in Ripley and was Head Teacher for the next 30 years. Mr Vincent and Miss Barker managed the evacuees as a separate unit. The staff had to organise free play and dinners in the holidays for the children whose mothers were involved with war work. The children took part in Warship Week in 1942 and Wings for Victory week in 1943, a book salvage drive in 1944 and a combined schools concert called 'Salute the Soldiers' in 1944. On the 23rd of June 1944 a flying bomb caused superficial damage to the school, which caused it to be temporarily closed. It was also closed on the 8th and 9th of May 1945, but this time the school log records it was because 'the war in Europe having come to an end, today is to be known as VE Day'.

SEND

An entirely new and very modern DISPENSARY has been installed in the Pharmacy of Kenneth E. White (late Allenby), Ripley. A full dispensing service is now available. All medical specialities are stocked here. Phone Ripley 111.—Advt.

For breaking the black-out on February 4th, Edith Mogilnicha, of Blacklands, Bush Lane, Send, was fined £3, at Woking on Saturday.

BONFIRE AT NIGHT.

At Woking on Saturday, Arthur James Davis, of Kildare, Send Marsh Road, Send, was fined £1 for displaying an external light during black-out on February 1st.—A constable gave evidence of finding a bonfire in defendant's garden and of assisting Mrs. Davis to put it out. The fire consisted of wood-shavings and sawdust.—Defendant said he had been burning a fire in a drum and at 5 p.m. he turned the whole lot out in the garden. When he went down just before 6 p.m. there was no fire, but to make sure he threw some wet stuff over it. It was all right when he left it.

'SALUTE THE SOLDIER' WEEK

Plans Going Forward

Plans for Send's 'Salute the Soldier' week, to be held on May 6th-May 13th, are fast taking shape. At a meeting of the Savings Committee, together with members co-opted from local organisations, held at St. Bede's Central School, Send, on Tuesday evening, a programme for the week was discussed. As previously stated, the target will be £17,500. Mr. B. J. Gay, headmaster of Send Central School, who presided, was elected chairman. Lieut. A. Sex, Home Guard, secretary, and Mr. Stokes, treasurer. Members of the committee at present constituted are Mr. Gay, Lieut. Sex, Mr. Stokes, Mrs. Martin, the Rev. D. G. Legg (the Vicar of Send), Mr. M. B. May, Miss Whitbourn, Miss Perrin (headmistress of Send Junior School), Mr. Wood, Mr. C. Ward, Mrs. Grantham and Miss Gardener.

It was decided to open three selling centres in the village. A grand opening procession through the village will be held on Saturday, May 6th, and a military display will take place in the school grounds, followed by a dance in the Drill Hall in the evening. A united service will be held in the Drill Hall on the Sunday afternoon. The programme for the rest of the week will include a cabaret and social on Monday, a whist drive at the Central School on Tuesday, a social and dance at the Drill Hall, organised by the Send Home Guard, on Wednesday, and an evening of music at the Central School on Thursday.

A united schools concert and operetta should prove a great attraction on the Friday, and the week will end with a play by the Home Guard on Saturday afternoon and a dance in the Drill

MEMORIES OF
VERA RASSELL

Another interesting memory is that of Vera Rassell, member of the Women's Land Army – WLA117452.

The Surrey History Centre in Woking has in its possession two wartime diaries, a photograph album and a letter from Mr Secrett all relating to the war service of Vera Rassell. Mr Secrett owned a large market garden in Send and land girls provided an important part of the workforce. The produce from market gardens such as Secrett's was vital at a time of food shortages.

Vera was living with other land girls at Tannery House in Send and the two diaries refer to her service during 1944 and 1945. The diaries are small commercial diaries and so each entry is short and written in pencil. Perhaps she had no time to read the papers or listen to the radio because she was working so hard, but it is interesting that most of the entries relate simply to her daily chores and pastimes. There is very little comment on the progress of the war itself, although this of course could also be due to an awareness of censorship, a lack of space in the diary or just that she preferred to screen out bad news. A typical entry might read, "Moved lettuce boxes all the morning. It turned out lovely - went shopping – finished my jumper off in the evening." or "Lettuce first thing then sweet corn. Did some

shopping. Went to Dunsfold. Had a drink. Went to a dance and had a good time."

There are some entries which refer to local wartime activities, for example, 13th April 1944 "Cabbage pulling first thing then rhubarb. Cycled to Woking. Watched some Americans play baseball." And 6th May "Salute the Soldier. We had a waggon in the procession with vegetables and won 1st prize. We sold them afterwards and made £14.12s.9d for the war effort." She also helped with other fund raising activities and took part in some Red Cross training. There is also the odd mention of soldiers leaving for active service "..Met Ted and George at the Seven Stars - kissed them goodbye"…

Whilst frozen leeks, brussels sprouts, sea kale, lettuces, etc., dominate the diaries, it is clear that Vera had time for some fun. Although on many evenings she knitted mittens, darned clothes, and even cut up a pair of old breeches and made them into shorts, wrote to friends and family or washed her hair, more exciting leisure activities were often logged. For example dances, "a dance with Twink – had a lovely time…", a snowball fight, trips to the pictures and in both years she managed a holiday to Bournemouth and a trip over to Ryde in the Isle of Wight.

On the 6th January 1944 "Had a grand party thanks to Mrs Dockerty. 24 of us played murders, dancing and games." Mrs Dockerty gets several positive mentions in the diaries but the most poignant is on January 3rd in the following year, when she notes "Bill Dockerty crashed and was killed" and then " Did sea kale all day. Felt pretty rotten hearing all about Bill." By January 7th Mrs Dockerty was back at work.

The entry for early May 1945 was surprisingly low key "Went to work. Peace was declared. Wrote to Doug. Cut lettuce. Planted Mint" However they did get a five-day holiday, which must have been welcome. On 24th May she notes she has been in the Land Army for two years and she received a new uniform and a two-year armband. Of course the girls could not be demobbed immediately because food was still short and it took time for soldiers returning from active duty to resume employment on the land. In fact in April 1945 she mentions that German prisoners of war filled part of the manpower shortage.

We get the occasional hint of how Vera felt about her employer, there are a few entries mentioning 'Nanny' being in a mood or a rotten mood. Mr Secrett was apparently known as Nanny because of his goatee beard. We do know how he felt about her from the warm farewell letter that has survived. Mr Secrett wrote to her from Heath Farm, when she left in March 1946. He talks of her

Vera Rassell and a friend in the onion field at Secretts

'loyal service', her 'example in setting standards of behaviour' and says 'I am sure I must have been trying at times but the quiet endeavour to put things right by you all soon pacified me. Here again I could sense your influence.' And finally he wished her well and enclosed some 'notes in appreciation of your work and example'. This gives a more positive impression of her 'boss' than some of the other wartime recollections that have been recorded!

MORE MEMORIES
FROM RIPLEY

Events in Ripley were obviously not so different from Send, although it had more housing and shops than Send at that time. Ripley, too, suffered bombing and the most often recalled event seems to be that concerning Tom Buller. Jack Smithers, for one, told Jane Bartlett in 1988, that Tom Buller, when bombed, landed in his bed in a crater and he was lodging with Mrs Burdett, a widow, in Newark Lane at the time. Jack added that his father was a firewatcher in the war. However we also have Tom's own account: he lived in various different lodgings and rented accommodation in Ripley. His first home was in Bonfield Terrace with Alan Grover, the driver of Collins grocery van, and he also lived in Bridgefoot Cottage and Rippleby Cottage (opposite Ripley House). He was living in Little Horrells when it was bombed and he 'came to' in a bomb crater instead of his bed, with a chimney pot resting against his head!

Tom Buller remembered that the Tannery was still working and beyond the Tannery was Fords, which made soles for boots and shoes during the War. It has since burnt down.

Tom served in the NFS (National Fire Service) during the war. There was a common joke that NFS people cycling back from Wisley or Vickers used to say to each other, "We could do with a bit of overtime, we're a bit short, there'll just be time to have tea before we're called out" and they would "chuck a fag down". On those occasions there was a series of little fires! They would have a relay of pipes from Boldermere to Wisley Common. "Pencil" Brown used to crawl through the pipe under the road to get the hose across. Tom did the driving but he often forgot the tender was a trailer and it bucketed about so much he nearly overturned it and all the "blokes" were hanging on and shouting.

He remembers "Turp" Giles was a fireman at Send and there was an NFS unit based in the garage at the Manor House, Send, when Gordon Stewart was there. In it were Stewart's and Secrett's men mainly, including Bert Hacker, Reg Tidy, Baigent, Dick Whitton and Reg Mussell. During the War Stewart's chicken farm was taken over by the Army and they stored foodstuffs in the chicken batteries. Peter Rixon recalled that just before 'D-Day' several of the older and stronger Send school boys were made to sign the Official Secrets Act and then they loaded up the lorries with bully beef etc. as the emergency supplies.

Alice Charman's husband, Jack, worked for Conisbee's for over 20 years first at East Horsley, then at Ripley. He had to

Gordon Stewart at the kennels in Send Marsh where the NFS was based

collect the wood for burning the bristles and was the bullock slaughterman. He also had to cut up and deliver. During the War his job was slaughterman for animals injured from the bombing. He was also in the Gas Contamination Squad, which checked the meat was safe for consumption. Both were reserved occupations. Although his health excused him, he did join the Home Guard and eventually he was called up and sent overseas.

Alice recalled that although in the War they theoretically had ration books, the grocers often wouldn't let them have food, "Had to save something for the gentry". Often the shops had nothing, but when her father was sent back from the front, he went and tackled the shops and said, "Don't give me that!"

The first bomb Alice remembered was on a Tuesday in 1940. It came down over the Charman's house in Newark Lane and April Cottage on to Little Horrells. Mike Collyer and his mother were taken out of April Cottage, all blood and soot. Mr Collyer was on Red Cross duty and his own house was the first house he was called to. They had just finished putting in everyone's doors and windows, including hers, when a week later on the Saturday bombs fell on Chapel Farm, the High Street and Horrells. That was when Tom Buller was blown out with bed and all into a crater. They carried him into the shelter at the bottom of Roy Baker's garden.

The day a doodlebug fell in Newark Lane the next-door neighbours had asked Alice in but she said no. She

A meaty subject...

She needs as much meat as he does!

and her neighbour dived into her cupboard (36 Newark Lane) and the place was filled with dust while the neighbours' house was hit. Later Tom Gunner erected shelters for people. The Charmans' shelter has recently been moved to the Send and Ripley History Society's museum but there is still one other in situ.

Mrs Ivy Wilkinson, née Smithers, gave an interview in 2005 to Jane Bartlett which included some of her wartime memories, including a story about the Newark Lane shelters. She was married and pregnant and living with her parents at 30 Newark Lane. Initially they shared a shelter with the Bakers, who lived next door at 32, but later they were given an Anderson shelter, which they had to erect themselves. Father Smithers used to stand on top of the shelter after an air raid warning. When he heard or saw danger he would call his family. The shelter had benches fitted each side and Grandfather Grace, Dolly Baker (née

Grace), Roy Baker and possibly two children plus Ivy and her parents would all squeeze in. It was very cold and there was no room for a heater. Mrs Smithers usually brought a saucepan of soup and poured it out into bowls. Ivy jumped so much when the guns went off from the Broadmead that she never drank her soup.

She said it was while they were down in the shelter that four of the six Horrells cottages were bombed and Tom Buller was rescued from the garden of the Horrells (he was a lodger of Ivy's aunt, Sarah Burdett). She recalled he was brought over and treated by ambulance men in the Bakers' shelter. The end almshouse in Newark Lane was also bombed and destroyed but luckily the Anscombes were staying away that night.

Pea Pod Soup

Wash the pods thoroughly and place in a deep saucepan. Add 2 sprigs of mint, 1 large potato, and chives, onion or spring onion (if available), a good pinch of salt and pepper, and cover with boiling water. Cook with the lid on until tender. Rub the vegetables and the pods through sieve, then return to the saucepan. Blend a little flour (1 oz to each pint) with cold water, add some of the hot soup to it. Return all to the saucepan and stir until boiling and the soup is creamy. Serve very hot.

Their cat crawled alive from the rubble. However, all the windows and doors were blown out of their row of cottages again.

During the War Lutidine House in Newark Lane was a hostel for difficult evacuee girls. Fred Dixon, the headmaster of the village school, recalled he also had evacuees from Fulham and Portsmouth. He also remembered that following some of the bombing the homeless were temporarily housed in the Church Hall.

Fred and Arthur Milton, like Mr Charman, were also in the butchery business. Rusts, a Ripley butchers, had a slaughter house until after the war, then the smaller ones were closed down, but there were still some larger ones left open. They used Frank Conisbee's in East Horsley and one in Dorking. Before Rusts was closed down, other butchers used to rent it on non-slaughter days; they usually slaughtered once a week. During the war the Home Guard spent a night in the pens, lit by hurricane lamps. Many were sick in the morning but they were not sure whether the lamps or the blood caused this.

Mr Rust was the agent for a house in Portsmouth Road. In the war Fred Milton was away in the forces and his wife went back to Lincolnshire with the kids, but when Rust got them the house she had to come back to put up curtains or they would have lost the house as being unoccupied.

In 1986 Betty Baker of Ripley also recorded some memories of her working life and she remembered that she left school at fourteen and worked for 37 years for W.B. Green. She went there during the War and as men were called up she found herself doing all sorts of duties including bookkeeping and accounts. Mr Green took her once a month to Guildford when they tried to call her up and said he couldn't manage to work without her and she kept getting a monthly reprieve.

Betty Baker's family have long been associated with the Ripley bonfire but she recalled that during the war there was no bonfire. Mrs Rose Bird, née Townsend, also had memories of war work. She worked at Vickers in both the 1st and 2nd World Wars doing engineering, but her mother worried about the bombing, so Dr. Ralli Creet managed to get her off the work for "health reasons." Ripley Court had become an annexe of Westminster Hospital and needed three local girls to help - odd jobs, mending, and helping with babies. Rose also helped look after two nursing sisters in the cottage right next door to her. She worked with Alice Carter (Ivy Sopp's elder sister) and they used to cycle to Guildford with Alice for cinema and dances. Her brother Harry (a POW in WWI) lived in the cottage which was replaced later by the bank building opposite W.B.Green's and her brother Robert first moved into the next door cottage (then empty) and later to Rippleby cottages. During the war they took sleeping bags and rugs when the sirens sounded and went up into fields at Grove Heath because of the worry of living in a wooden cottage.

Mr and Mrs Herbert Brown commented on the wartime change in the use of Ripley Court School. The boys having been evacuated to Wales, the school became a maternity hospital. The doctors boarded with the vicar, the Rev. Thomas at the Vicarage, and apparently the Browns used to hear them running up Rose Lane to the school at night when there was a confinement. Dr Ralli Creet, a Greek, was the local doctor. He lived next to The Georgian House in the High Street, on the Guildford side. Mrs Brown also remembered Ostlers Cottages in Rose Lane having red crosses on all the doors during World War 2 because they were bug-infested and had to be fumigated.

Grace Blackman was another who remembered wartime work. She came fresh from college to be the infant teacher at Ockham School, teaching children between four and nine years old. Winifred Wilby was the head teacher and had the older children (there were only two teachers). She started on the day war broke out (1939) and the headmistress said "All our teachers go to The Ship." Mother worried! Mrs Billinghurst greeted her at the pub with, "We are all ready for you." Her room

was on the 1st floor over the street, and the sitting room was halfway down the stairs. She remembered that everything shone, every brass door handle and all the copper in the bar. The passageway to the back (now incorporated) was white hearthstone and scrubbed by Lally, their daughter, every morning. The brass doorknobs often wore out. After closing time the whole place was cleaned out. For a time there was one other lodger, the young male teacher from Ripley. She had full board and lovely meals and was there for three years.

At a period of bombing and bomb scares in World War 2, thirteen people slept in the bar, thinking the heavy beams were protection. Some put their heads under the elm tables – apparently amongst them was Mr Richardson from the sweet shop, and the manager of the International Stores.

Audrey Brown, née Chandler, worked at the telephone exchange in the last house in Ryde Close, Chestnut Cottage. This only took up the front room and the rest of the house was lived in by Mrs Baker, who acted as caretaker. Audrey was supposed to start work there, aged sixteen. There were four girls and a supervisor. She worked there for ten years, as did Audrey Dye (Mrs Baker's daughter). After hours Mrs Baker answered the phone. During the war the windows were sandbagged for safety and the Home Guard made it a priority. It was closed after the War although, when Gerald Chandler later lived there, it still had metal plates for the switchboard bolted to the floor of the front room. On VE Day Mrs Baker sent the girls off to the pub, and said she would hold the fort. Although they were not allowed to listen in, they had a good idea of many of the activities in the village and had to be careful to remember whether they had really been told something or had merely 'gathered' it!

The telephone exchange was close to the Green, which Sir Oliver Simmonds of Dunsborough House was allowed to plough during the war. Bracken and gorse on the Green made way for corn, and it was then re-grassed after the war. Betty Nokes said that they kept the ancient right to hold a fair on the Green alive, by having a coconut shy at the back of W.B.Green's shop.

One of the most interesting episodes of the war in Ripley was the early use of penicillin. Fred Dixon, the headmaster of the school recalled that the chemist's

The Ripley Pharmacy, which has since closed

shop sold eggs, dog biscuits and birdseed until Ken White came. Jack Ellard told the Society that he used to come and visit Ken White during the war (Jack was stationed in Portsmouth Naval Hospital). Ken had taken over the management of the pharmacy c.1943 for Mrs Allenby, when her brother-in-law Harry, the chemist, died. He only had the present shop (now the Ceramic Café). The back dispensing room was then a little sitting room, and all dispensing was done behind a screen. He then acquired the sitting room as well and cleared it out and converted it. There was no running water, all dispensing being done with bowls of water. Previously the shop had cabbages, junk jewellery, everything but medicine. Jack thought Ken was mad, particularly when he said he was going to produce penicillin. Penicillin was controlled under the Official Secrets Act, but he obtained some culture and the formula from someone (he never said who). The inspectors came down and said he couldn't but Ken said he knew how. He only made penicillin cream ointment for vets, as he had no licence. It was in great demand and he begged Jack to join him as he was run off his feet.

After the war Jack came in (c.1946) and they made a mini sterile room, with an aperture through which to put rubber-gloved hands. The Ministry of Health came down to see what they were up to. Jack scrubbed, polished and dusted and talked about his time in naval hospitals and they granted them a licence. Then they made frozen crystals in little glass tubes, to use for human injections, which were in great demand at local hospitals. He even took some in a vacuum flask when he went to the pictures as he was often called out for emergencies.

Other war work went on locally as Sid Stanley has recalled. Behind Fisher's Garage on the Portsmouth Road, May and Hardy made screws for the aircraft industry. At Burnt Common during the war Mr Oliver's premises were used as a Dispersal Unit from Fairoaks, Chobham. Many of the skilled aircraft workers were sent to work in small groups away from their main centre of Fairoaks in case of direct hits. Those working on the ground floor repaired aeroplane wings of Blenheims and Beauforts. The neighbouring tearoom (the smaller building with a weather vane) was their canteen. Gerald Chandler recalled that at Wisley aerodrome the bombers took off over Battleston Hill to be tested. The noise and vibrations were such that lessons at school stopped and roofs rattled. John Paul also had connections with Wisley. He was in the Home Guard, which was formed about 1941, and they used to march round Wisley aerodrome. They were issued with live ammunition, save for one man and he wasn't allowed live ammunition if there was a full moon! They often did combined exercises with, or against, Byfleet Home Guard. John and his adjutant were given a training course on camouflage and more sophisticated weapons so they were considered the platoon experts. One night Byfleet had the "enemy" camp on top of Cockrow Hill, Wisley. John and

Ripley Home Guard

his adjutant were told to recce and find the strength of the camp and report back. They crawled on all fours for hours, froze, as they had been taught, at the slightest sound but finally they got so tired that they walked boldly into the camp, counted heads, were ignored by the "enemy" and walked back to the main road. There was no one there - their men had got bored with waiting and had gone home.

On another exercise the whole platoon was late crawling up to the aerodrome. They had found a field of mushrooms, and they had all filled their tin hats. They used to practise with live ammunition and live grenades on the common but were terrified of hitting courting couples (they did fly a danger flag.) They also practised at Bisley on the Byfleet range with .22s and .303s. John Paul found

it amazing how one sedate Ripley man shed his inhibitions as soon as he had his uniform on and was with the others when they whistled after all the girls.

The headquarters of the Home Guard was in the Talbot ballroom. It was a hard floor to sleep on. Dick Lillywhite also remembered the Home Guard headquarters behind the Talbot in the hall. One day he said the VIPs were coming and they had their sentries all out in front to give them warning, but the 'big-wigs' suddenly stepped in - they hadn't come in that way, but round the back!

Betty Mussell worked at the Talbot during the war. The Canadians were billeted in Ockham Park and they used to bring blackmarket carcasses and cigarettes at night. It was difficult as the dining room was full and the cook was busy. The police and wardens were doing their rounds, so they used to pop in and out to watch for the police and then they used to slip out to the yard to help unload. Mr Tickner was an easygoing warden, but Doug White was a stickler for having everything correct.

John Paul also said that the Home Guard dug tank traps on the Green and put sandbags round houses. The blocks, which are still around Ryde House, were originally put up as tank obstructions. He always marched behind Haines who was a huge man with big feet, who marched more slowly than the rest. Mr Paul became hypnotized by it and found himself tending to match Haines' steps as well. The safest place to be when Haines was firing was where he was aiming, which was odd since he was a poacher by trade and an absolute deadly shot with a catapult. They first had aged rifles but NCOs later had Sten guns, which they found much lighter to carry. Great fun.

John Paul remembered three sergeants – Hooker, Stocker and Williams. Apparently Sergeant Williams was so unpopular that he got pushed into the duckweed of the pond. John Paul was originally in the Civil Defence in Ripley. The post was in the shed behind the chemist's shop. One of their jobs was to distribute air raid warnings to minor posts. There was a siren on the roof of the Fire Station. They had to ring Mr Collins, the baker, to sound the alarm. One night they rang him – a long silence

- they rang him again. "Oh, I forgot," he said, and the Ripley alarm sounded the alert just after all the neighbouring villages sounded the all clear. After that the Ripley siren was moved.

When the bombs fell in Newark Lane, the warden came out shaking like a leaf. "The whole house is alive with ferrets." Mr Gribble, the farmer, went in and came out with ferrets between the fingers of his very large hands. The bombs he remembered in Ripley were the one in Newark Lane destroying Little Horrells, the one in the High Street, opposite the garage and the one at Burnt Common as well as one in Rose Lane at the gateway to Chapel Farm (later to become the Baden-Powells' house). For the Rose Lane bomb, John Paul had been patrolling with Gribble; he heard the bomb flaps open and ran down Rose Lane expecting to see his house ruined (Apple Trees). He met a dog rushing up the opposite way with his tail between his legs and found it was the house next door to him instead. Dorothy Colborn also suffered from the bombing. When their house was bombed, her mother was in her 80s and they had to climb out over the rubble. It was an eighteenth century cottage and compensation was what an old cottage would fetch in an auction, so they only got a few hundred, and that was after the war. Their rescued furniture and possessions were put in a farm house, Upton Farm at Ockham, but the rats got most of it. They stayed with cousins in Effingham until Miss Farr (who owned a lot of property) had a cottage fall vacant next to Miss Baker's.

Basil Howard in a 1983 letter to Bob Gale mentioned bomb damage to the corner property now known as the Cedar House. He said that when his parents eventually moved back to Yorkshire, they then let the Cedar House (now called Tudor House) to a Mr and Mrs Burnside as a private dwelling, and let the corner tea house, (originally a butcher's shop) to Mysie Taplin as a tea house, both shortly before WWII. During the war some damage was sustained to the front of the houses by a bomb which exploded in the road outside. After the war Basil's parents sold both houses, Miss Taplin having given up the tea house and taken the Rendezvous Café in Guildford. The corner house became a restaurant, and the now Tudor House remained a private dwelling.

Mr and Mrs George Best of Newark Lane set down their memories in 1986. In the little wooden snack bar called Weirside on the road opposite Newark

Mill they made homemade ice cream in a bucket with ice and salt and a handle that turned the container. Things ran

down during the war when supplies were low, and the Ministry of Health stopped it after the war as there was no running water and they used to get their water from the Mill. Elsie Best, née Plumbridge, said that the mill did not have much land, only the pasture running back behind the mill, where they grew a hay crop and they had some pigs for their own use during the war. Mr Best was invalided out of Navy before the war with an injured back and worked at Vickers and was also in the Auxiliary Fire Service.

Kathleen Lloyd, née Giles, went away to be a housekeeper for two years and then married. When World War 2 came, her husband Peter joined the army so she came back home to look after her father in Rose Lane. Her dad was also in the Fire Service and an air raid warden and doing carpentry work for Reg Allwork. He dug graves and helped in the British Legion, particularly in the bar. Many Canadian soldiers came to the Legion and father would bring them back afterwards to doss down for the night all over the cottage. The Drill Hall in Send was the centre for recreation for the forces in Send; Ripley had the British Legion in Rose Lane. Victor Weller, Chairman of the Legion in 1987, recalled how they sent packets of cigarettes to prisoners of war when they were in Germany in World War 1, and comfort parcels in World War 2. They gave you a welcome-back parcel when you came home on leave and they did a lot of welfare and benevolent work. Mr Gadd, when he was secretary 1939-49,

A football team outside the British Legion in Rose lane

had a list in his office of all the local men, and when they were on leave they all came in to see him.

Not all wartime memories were sombre ones as Archie Marsh can testify. He said his wartime memories were all laughs. He was helping Pat Fox's father collect chickens for market one night when the warning went that doodlebugs were coming over. When the engine of one of them stopped and its dive started, they dropped the crate of chickens and both dived for cover in a wire chicken run and then realized how futile it was.

Another time on his way up Newark Lane with Tom Buller, for ARP duty, some bombs fell. He dived to one side of Stan Perrin's wall and Tom dived to the other side. He had his hat on but poor Tom did not! Tom Buller was the one who was bombed in Little Horrells. According to Archie, he and his bed landed in a crater and his watch was on the bed head still ticking! Gribble was the Warden that night and he picked up the ferrets from next door, held one up, looked at it and said – "Oh, he has

some teeth on him, the varmint." It is interesting that most of the locals recall the plight of poor Tom Buller but each time the details vary! The ARP Warden's post on the Green was where the Over 60's Club met. Biz Bashall (of Wentworth Cottages, part of the Lovelace Estate) was on warden duty. They were all playing cards for money when they heard Charlie Nokes's footsteps doing the rounds. They tried to hide the cards and money, as he was a very moral man. Another night when a doodlebug came over, Biz, a very peaceable and quiet man, stood there muttering "Go on you bugger, go on you bugger" on and on until it had passed. He had no idea he was saying it.

The Ripley Home Guard on the green

The night the incendiaries came down in Newark Lane, all the way from Hedgecroft to the Seven Stars and in the fields opposite, was like a firework night. (Pat Fox's home was behind the Seven Stars.) There were incendiaries all over the road and the fire engine driver just drove through them. They tried to move all cars and other vehicles but it was a winter night and they were all frozen solid. One incendiary fell into the larder of the Seven Stars; the cowshed of Homewood Farm was on fire and the hoses were too short to reach so they had to run with buckets of water. The Rev. Thomas stood like a gawp just in the way, between where they filled the buckets and ran to the fire, so one of them dashed past on one side and he swung round to look as another man brushed past on his other side, then he tried to swing round again but slipped on the ice and fell flat. That got him out of

VE Day aprty on Georgelands

the way. Bob Brewer was standing on a shed with a stirrup pump when the main fire engine came and the hose caught him and he went flying. At one stage they discovered to their horror that it was a churn of milk they were tipping on to the flames by accident. Pat's brother in his new Home Guard's uniform was shovelling up incendiaries that had not ignited (he took them to work and defused them – he still has one.) When his new trousers were dried they had

shrunk and it was Church Parade next morning – so he did not go!

Bev Jackman added to our wartime stories in 1991 when she recalled her school days in Ripley. When there was an air raid, a buzzer in the police station was pressed, which could be heard in the school and the children went to the shelters. Apparently Mr Dixon, the headmaster, was hard of hearing and sometimes the boys would say the buzzer had gone so they could avoid Maths! They were told not to pick up the anti-radar silver paper but they did and they took it to school and swapped it for other things like bits of shrapnel. There was also a gardening club behind the police station and Bev had hurt her foot when a fork fell on it so she missed the VE Day celebrations but she remembered celebrations outside The Anchor and local street parties.

Bev's grandparents had a smallholding in Polesden Lane and they grew brussels sprouts. One night a lot of incendiary bombs lit up the sky like fairy lights and her grandfather was upset to find the sprouts cooked on the stalks. One bomb dropped on the road in new tarmac and bounced into the garden but left an impression on the road and all but said 'love from Hitler'. They had an Anderson shelter in the garden, which was used by four families. They had bunk beds in it and as children they had the time of their lives in there. She said that as a child a lot that happened seemed to be fun and she did not really realise that people were being hurt. On one occasion an anti-aircraft gun was in their driveway and when it fired at a plane it blew in their windows and doors. She recalled the doodlebugs and how there was uncertainty and panic when their engines cut out, as it was not known which way they would fall. She remembered watching planes in the beam of searchlights and also a German plane coming down in Ockham. The pilot was brought to Ripley Police station and lots of women spat at him and she thought this was awful. On a nicer note there were POWs at Homewood Farm who made her little carved toys.

The following article, compiled by Tony and John Milton, was printed in the Society's Journal 197 and appeared after this collection was put together, hence its position in the book.

BERTHA AND HER BOYS

William Milton was born in Thursley in Surrey in 1883. His father was an estate worker for Lloyd George at Witley Park, but he died when William was just 13. William (Bill) joined the Surrey Constabulary, initially at Dorking where, in June 1909, he met and married Bertha Joyes, and following a spell in Chertsey, was transferred to Ripley as a police constable. At first they lived in Amberly cottage, (opposite The Anchor), and later moved to Rippleby Cottages at the northern end of the High Street. By the time war was declared in 1939, Bill and Bertha had eight children, five boys and three girls; the war was to affect them all in various ways.

THE BOYS

Their eldest son was Herbert William (Bill); he joined the 6th Battalion of the Grenadier Guards and was posted to North Africa as part of General Montgomery's 8th Army advance into Tunisia. In the battle of 'The Mareth Line' they were the first to meet the enemy after the evacuation of Dunkirk and suffered heavy casualties. Bill was an Officer's batman and on the 17th March 1943 (his 33rd birthday) he was severely wounded by shrapnel, his officer was killed and Bill was taken prisoner of war (Prisoner of War No.8493). He

was transported overland to a Prisoner of War hospital in Italy, but when the Germans surrendered in North Africa, he was moved to Poland, Austria, Czechoslovakia and Russia, spending most of his time in Prisoner of War Camp 'Stalag 18A'. Meanwhile Bertha, Bill's wife Bessie and daughter Sheila received a telegram, 'Missing, presumed killed in action'. It was a further two years before they were eventually told that he was being held in Stalag 18a.

Charlie left his job as chauffeur and gardener to Lord and Lady Bray to join the RAF where he became a corporal in the RAF police (later the RAF Regiment) He was stationed at various bases in Essex with 11 Group Fighter Command including Hornchurch, Foulness Island and North Weald where he was attached to a Norwegian squadron. He also served at Westhampnett (Goodwood) and briefly at Tangmere. Towards the end of the war he was posted to Germany but had to return home due to ill health.

Fred joined the Royal Artillery as a driver. He was involved in the 'big push' through France, Belgium and Germany, arriving in Hamburg shortly after it was bombed. He was involved in transferring German POWs to Bavaria by train.

Towards the end of the war he played football for the BLA (British Liberation Army) in Belgium. On his return he found he had contracted TB. After a year being nursed at home he was placed in Redhill Hospital and then Milford Isolation Hospital where he had a lung removed.

Arthur (Tonnie) was the second youngest boy, and being just 16 when war was declared he initially joined the Home Guard. In August 1941 he enlisted in the Armoured Division based at Bovingdon, only to be sent home again as he was still a month off his 18th birthday. In October that year he joined the Gloucester Regiment as an infantryman and after training in communications he was transferred to the Royal Navy on HMS Royal Arthur at Skegness (on the site of a Butlins Holiday Camp) to complete his training as a Royal Navy Signalman. He was posted to the Middle East on HMS Ajax, a Leander-class Light Cruiser, and from there to HMS Nile based in Alexandria, where on the 16th June 1944 he married Helen Ward, a switchboard operator with the ATS, whom he met on a blind date. Helen was attached to the shore base and was originally from Willesden in North London.

John was the baby of the family, being only 8 when the war commenced. During school holidays he worked at Dunsborough Farm helping with the harvest, or at Gribbles Farm (Rose Lane) potato picking. He was to remain at home with Bill and Bertha and his sisters until the end of the war. He remembers the nights spent in their Morrison shelter (a steel indoor table shelter), of exploding doodlebugs and captured German airmen being held at the Doctor's Surgery. After the war he played professional football for Southend United and Exeter City, before emigrating to Australia in 1970.

RPL.71 HIGH STREET, RIPLEY

At the end of the war all the boys returned to live and work in Ripley. Bill's was an emotional homecoming, especially for mum Bertha and his wife and daughter. Later he separated from Bessie and married Maisey Elliott from Ockham, and became the curator at Clandon Park House for Lord Onslow. Charlie married Eunice Irene Cradduck (Rene) from Cranbrook, Kent. Rene and Charlie met when he was getting a lift back to base in the back of a three-ton truck. She had joined the WRAF on return from a holiday in Germany on the first day war was declared! She promptly trained as a Plotter in the Ops Room at Hornchurch where she served during the Battle of Britain. Later, Rene trained at RAF Cranwell as a Radar Operator and was posted to Beachy Head, Eastbourne. On his return to Ripley, Charlie went to work for the GPO at Woking. Fred married Divina Smith from Lincolnshire a month before being called up in July 1940, after meeting on a Ripley British Legion outing to Littlehampton with Bland's Coaches. Divina worked at Vickers in the Wing Department before it was bombed. Both Fred and Arthur worked for Rust's Butchers when they returned (next to Weller's bakery where Seymour Estate Agents are now) with younger brother John as delivery boy. They opened Milton Bros Butchers, initially in West Horsley, and later they opened a shop in Ripley (next to the current Post Office).

THE GIRLS

Anne was the eldest daughter; she worked in the International Stores in Ripley. She met David Slessor, a Captain in the Canadian Army who was based at Ockham Park. Dave was promoted to Major shortly before the D-Day landings. They married in 1945, and after the birth of their first son, David, left

England to live in Ottawa, where Dave was to become the Surveyor General of Canada.

Elsie met another Canadian serviceman, Cecil Dares, at a dance in the Talbot Hotel; he was also posted to Ockham Park along with his brother Gordon. Cecil, Gordon and Dave Slessor were part of the Royal Canadian Engineers survey and mapping unit, and were involved in the support team to follow the D-Day landings. Cecil and Elsie married in 1946 and left England to live in Nova Scotia where Cecil was a fish warden and forestry worker.

Joyce, the youngest daughter, worked with her sister Elsie at May and Hardy's factory near Burnt Common (behind Fishers garage) making engineering components for the war effort (Masser May was later to become CO of Send

Flight ATC). Joyce married John Davis, a First Officer in the Merchant Navy and they lived with Bill and Bertha at Rippleby Cottages.

As for Bill Milton (Snr), during the war years he was a volunteer fireman and fire-watcher (looking out for fires after an air-raid). He was employed by Surrey County Council building and maintaining roads. This also included the two aircraft runways at Wisley and Dunsfold. He was chairman of the Ripley Football Club and the Tontine Club (a Christmas savings club) and he took over from his son Charlie as part-time gardener for Sir Jocelyn Bray. Meanwhile Bertha had the house to run, which was by now home to her extended family. She had her daughters' weddings to arrange and she had to wait, as mothers do, for the safe return of 'her boys.'

The Canadians in Ockham Park, Gordon Dares, Dave Slessor and Cecil Dares

MEMORIES OF
MICHAEL MORRIS

Michael Morris was nearly four years old at the outbreak of the war and lived in a bungalow called Jesmond Dene on what is now known as Potters Lane, Send, but which Michael knew as Cartbridge Lane. His parents both came from Hull – his father had come to Send to operate a dredger on the Wey for a Hull-based company called Priestmans that built cranes and dredgers. Initially he had lodged with Mr and Mrs Skipper but moved into rented accommodation probably in Papercourt Lane after he was married at Send Church. By the time Michael was born in 1935 they had moved to Potters Lane and he thinks the bungalow was a new build and named after a place near Newcastle.

Michael was the eldest of three – his brother Keith was four years younger and his sister, Doreen, eight years his junior. The age difference meant they were not really his playmates, but Michael was never short of friends as the surrounding houses had many children of his age. The Norman family had four children, as did the Gibbs Family, and the Ingrams had two daughters, Rita and Margaret. There were also Lorrie Parsons and the Marshalls in Briar Road. Apparently, less desirable playmates were Jimmy Wells (not approved of by his mother) and Miss Lumley, (thought to be 'stuck up'!). Local children walked across the fields,

past Baigent's farm, to the school, and although a bright boy Michael was often up to mischief. When not in school, the boys played in the road or in the fields and sandpits, roaming free, occasionally pursued by the local 'ogres', Fred and Jim Oliver and Jimmy Riddle (or at least that is what he was known as). Jim Oliver chased them once from the seat by the big oak tree on Potters Lane into the field where they hid in a haystack.

Potters Lane had very little traffic so hopscotch and rounders could be played in the road. When the 'winkleman' came round on his bicycle, selling seafood, the children would stop playing and sit on the kerb and use pins to get the winkles out. Although traffic was light, Michael had one close shave when he was coming down the hill on his homemade go-kart and had to swerve to avoid an oncoming car, ending up in a patch of stinging nettles. His suffering received no sympathy at home! The fields opposite his house, known as the Broomfields, full of broom and gorse, were an ideal area for cowboys and indians using bows and arrows, but the highlight of the area seems to have been the ponds and sandpits that lay behind his house.

The sandpits were not worked at this time and were a great area to make camps. The dreaded Jimmy Riddle, 'a figure out of Pickwick, the bane of our lives' acted as caretaker of the sandpits and attempted to frighten the boys off by waving a stick and shouting at them. Part of the attraction of the workings was a concrete structure that resembled a castle which had been used for grading the sand and gravel. The boys used catapults and had stone fights and amazingly no one got seriously hurt. Occasionally boys such as Bernard Moore and Henry Ray from a rival Wharf Lane gang came to take them on. Another attraction was the ponds, one of which had a sandy beach where they made sandcastles and sailed small boats. The Canadian soldiers played a trick on them on one occasion when they encouraged the boys to cross a pontoon bridge onto a small island and then swung the bridge

Michael and Keith 'on active service'

away, leaving them stranded. Michael's love of flowers got him into trouble when he attempted to pick yellow irises from the edge of the pond for his mother. He got in deeper and deeper and eventually lost a shoe, not popular when clothing was on coupons. Michael dared not go home until he heard a search party looking for him. He got a strapping for his prank.

Initially Michael's mother had been in service at Hoe Place School but by the war she worked at Sendholme. This had several benefits for the young Michael – the family had produce, including grapes, from the estate and he was allowed to explore the grounds. He saw little of Miss Lancaster but he remembers the gardener, Mr Bugg, the chauffeur, Ron Jackman and the cook, Mrs Jackman, who made macaroni cheese that could be eaten in slices. Michael's mother was rather proper and although Michael was christened at Send Church, he attended Sunday school at the church at Cartbridge. At about the age of eight or nine Michael's mother bought him his first grey flannel suit (still short trousers), which he wore to Sunday school. On the way home he was tempted by the offer of hot sausages to go and sit on an oil drum in the Canadians' camp – unfortunately it was not a very clean oil drum and once again he was in trouble!

Towards the end of the war Michael remembers convoys parking up in Potters Lane overnight. Some of the Canadians had a tented camp in Potters Lane and tested their amphibious vehicles in the run up to D-Day.

One incident that Michael thinks he never told his mother concerned the river. This was a happy place to spend time, playing in inner tubes at Triggs Lock, watching barges carrying wood and coal and sometimes trying to beg or borrow a boat from Geoffrey Groves —occasionally successfully. One time he was accompanied by Tony Davis, a ginger haired boy, when two ladies in a skiff hailed them, who offered the boys a ride if they did the rowing. All went well until they reached a sandy bank near a lock when the ladies asked the boys if they were going to swim. The boys declined, having no swimming trunks, but the ladies had no such inhibitions and stripped off, causing Tony to turn as red as a beetroot.

Despite many happy times playing, Michael and his friends were aware of the war. Michael said his mother took in evacuees at various times despite only having two bedrooms, although he has little memory of them. He does remember bombers going over, and the sound of guns on the Broadmead. On one occasion when he was eating pudding at school they heard the siren, the bang of a buzz bomb and they dived under the trestle tables. When they emerged it looked like something from the Battle of the Somme with red jam,

custard, collapsed tables and broken plates everywhere (this sadly was the bomb that killed many of the Privett family).

School children were warned against picking up bits or pieces. Notwithstanding this, they collected or swapped and traded shrapnel, spent shells and chunks off planes which were hidden in hidey holes in the sandpits to keep them away from adult eyes. The adults would also probably not have approved that the Canadians gave them Sweet Caporal cigarettes in blue and white packets, which featured plane silhouettes inside the packaging, nor would he have liked his mother to have known he drank scrumpy provided by the West Country farm manager on the farm in Woodhill. Margaret Leighton, the actress, owned the farm and Michael used to help with the harvest, making the stooks. He also helped pick potatoes on the Duke of Sutherland's estate at Sutton Place, but unfortunately there was no scrumpy!

He also recalled some of the shops in Send: Gladdings Stores on the corner, Hesters the butchers, Oldlands, who sold fruit and veg, Broomfields the shoemakers and the Co-op, where his mother's divvy (dividend) number was 2086. The Send Post Office during the war was in Potters Lane and was run by Mr and Mrs Fielding. Their son Barry was not allowed to play with Michael and his friends and Barry went on to the Grammar School after the war. Michael also had the chance to go, but opted instead to go to Guildford Tech (much to his mother's disappointment) and then take up an apprenticeship at Vickers, following in his father's footsteps. Prior to the war his father had worked for Ron Sex at the forge but moved to Vickers during the war, which meant he could live at home. They raised chickens and rabbits in the back garden and Michael helped looked after them.

Michael more than once described his childhood as idyllic and certainly it sounds as though the war did nothing to stop him having a lot of fun.

Michael Morris emigrated to Canada and then to the United States, but returned to England where he ran the post office in Pyrford and now lives in Guildford.

VE Day scenes from London

John Hutson by a Gloucester Gladiator that made a
forced landing near Papercourt Lake.

ACKNOWLEDGMENTS

Many memories have gone to make up this book and the main contributors are
acknowledged in the text. Some of the contributors have also provided photographs,
and other photographs have come from the Send and Ripley History Society archive.
Please note that the overall copyright to this document resides with the Society.

Some of the accounts were summaries of what was told to the editor and these were
referred back to the person concerned for checking. Other accounts were written by
the people themselves and have generally been left unaltered. Needless to say after
many years there are discrepancies over details and so we hope readers will excuse
any inconsistencies.

However, some additional material has come from outside sources and we therefore
acknowledge recipes and pictures taken from 'We'll Eat Again' by Marguerite Patten.

Photograph of evacuees courtesy of edubuzz.org wwii learning notes.

Final page photos from Poppy Press (British Legion) anniversary addition.
Originally from the Imperial War Museum archive.

Newspaper extracts were taken from the Surrey Advertiser and the Manchester
Guardian.

INDEX